GHOST INVESTIGATOR

Volume 12

Written by
Linda Zimmermann

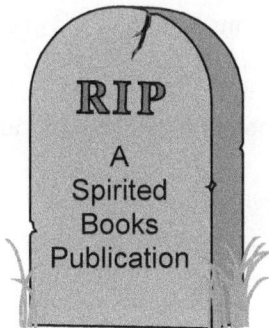

RIP

A
Spirited
Books
Publication

Linda Zimmermann's Facebook Fan Page

http://www.facebook.com/pages/Linda-Zimmermann/116636310250

The author is always looking for new ghost stories. If you would like to share a haunting experience or find out more about her work, go to:

www.ghostinvestigator.com

Or write to:

Linda Zimmermann
P.O. Box 192
Blooming Grove, NY 10914

Or send email to:

lindazim@optonline.net

What else is Linda Zimmermann writing? Go to: **www.gotozim.com**

Ghost Investigator: Volume 12

Copyright © 2014 Linda Zimmermann
Second Edition, September 2014

ISBN: 978-1-937174-25-5

CONTENTS

Websites:

Linda Zimmermann:
www.gotozim.com

Barbara Roth Bleitzhofer:
www.barbrothreadings.com

Michael Worden:
www.michaeljworden.com

Pine Bush House

This is another case that came my way as a result of meeting someone at one of the Pine Bush UFO Fairs, back in 2013. It was Barbara Grey, owner of the beautiful Pine Bush House bed and breakfast on Maple Street. Almost a year passed before she contacted me again, but once I heard some of her stories, I knew it was a place I had to visit.

The house was built in 1904 for Archibald Taylor, who was in real estate and the lumber business. *The History of Orange County New York*, published in 1908, had the following entry:

The growth of Pine Bush has been largely increased by the opening of the railroad...Mr. A.R. Taylor has taken a liberal course, as an owner of a large amount of real estate, in opening new streets and contributing largely to every measure of village improvement. He has been largely employed as a civil engineer and land surveyor, and is still often engaged in land surveys and the adjustment of boundaries. He drove the first railroad stake in Chicago during an engagement at the West many years ago.

Another entry describes the family and lumber business:

H. R. TAYLOR, of Pine Bush, N. Y., who conducts an extensive trade in lumber, building materials, etc., established this business in 1895. His father, Archibald R. Taylor, was a native of Ulster County, and in 1849 located in Pine Bush, where he purchased a large tract of land, and began the erection of buildings. He was largely identified with the prosperity of this village and associated with its business interests. In 1856 he married Miss Mary, daughter of John Colwell Rainey, of Crawford. The following children were born: Archibald, Hamilton R., Emily, Anne and John C., now state senator.

An early 1900s postcard image of the house.

The family was obviously prosperous and wielded considerable influence in the area, and their stately home naturally reflected their status. But the property was to undergo changes over the years, including several additions—additions which around 1980 became part of a senior housing facility. The large bedrooms in the main house were still occupied, but

2

only by those that could afford them. The less economically fortunate had tiny rooms that had been partitioned off in the dormitory addition.

Someone who worked there, who wanted to keep all names anonymous, wrote the following about the place:

I am a close friend of (names removed), *two previous owners. I lived in the bungalow with my children for a few years, and took care of people there for many years. Pine Bush House was an adult residence (mostly women) where lots of old folks, some with psychiatric problems, died.*

We did a lot of praying in that house for a lot of years. There was a lot of healing, a lot of deliverance. Many spiritual people living there. And I do believe some people were not at peace, and many died there. I just know (name removed) *was reluctant to ship them off to nursing homes. She loved them all, and put up with some very crazy people, so it made her job hard.*

This person also went on to name and describe many of the residents, both in terms of their physical characteristics, and personalities—as well as any mental illnesses from which they were suffering. I will maintain the privacy of these individuals even though they are deceased, but suffice it to say, there were enough issues and situations to create a whole host of confused and disturbed spirits. Whether or not the profiles of these individuals could be matched to any of the paranormal activity in the house remained to be seen.

The senior home operated for about 25 years, until it was converted to a bed and breakfast. When Barbara and her husband, Mark, bought the place, they lovingly restored it to its former glory. However, there are some things that nails and paint can't change—the remnants and imprints of the former residents. The following are just some of the things that Barbara has experienced over the years.

- *My husband and I live in the basement. Sometimes, at night, you can hear someone walking above us (the dining room/butler's pantry area is directly above our living room). It drives my husband crazy, and he insists it's one of our tenants walking up to her apartment in the back - but I've checked and she's not always home when it happens. Mark doesn't believe in spirits - he thinks Kodie (an employee at the B&B) and I are crazy.*

3

- *I have two small furbabies [dogs] that are a little over a year old. We were doing renovations in our basement kitchen in the fall when our girl, Tinkerbell, had an encounter of some kind. We had a pet gate up so the dogs couldn't get into the construction area. There are often times when Tinkerbell (it's always Tinkerbell, never her brother) will look into our bedroom and bark at the dark, or go to the bottom of the stairs (leading up to the kitchen) and bark. This night she kept going to the gate and barking - she wouldn't stop even after I started fussing at her (it was beginning to be annoying). I turned the light on to show her there was nothing there. After about an hour of the barking I heard a big crash - like something heavy fell over. Tinkerbell comes running through the living room and jumps on the couch shaking all over. I went to the kitchen area and couldn't find anything that had fallen over - everything was the same as I had left it. I went upstairs, but there weren't any issues up there. Tinkerbell wouldn't follow me - she stayed trembling in the corner of the couch. It took me about 30 minutes to get her semi calmed down - even then she got on the back of the sofa and hid behind me under my hair. She didn't make a sound the rest of the night.*

What does Tinkerbell see?

4

- *Another time I was in the dining room talking on the phone. I heard someone come down the front stairs, and the vestibule light turned on - a few seconds later it turned off, and I heard someone go back up the stairs. Thinking Kodie was here, I finished my conversation, went to the bottom of the stairs, and called out. After the third or fourth time I called her name, she comes walking in the front door - it hadn't been her, and I had been the only one in the house.*

- *I had only lived here about a year when I was sitting at the kitchen table making out menus for the coming weekend. I heard the front door open/close, and someone walking up the front stairs (same stairs as in the previous paragraph). Thinking it was Kodie's sister, I went out to meet her - it wasn't her, she wasn't even on her way over.*

- *For around 6 months or so, Mark and I lived on the third floor. I always had things happen up there - personal items being moved around, doors closing and being locked, etc. 95% of the guests who have asked if the house is haunted have done so based on what they've experienced on the third floor.*

- *There's a local lady who personally knew the previous owners (two sets ago) when this property was being run as a senior's home. She has all kinds of tales about "things" happening here. She immediately knew what I was talking about when I started asking her questions.*

- *I have an apartment in the back (long term rental) that housed some of the seniors during the time it was a senior home. The tenant would go through periods when she would come home to find her poor dog, Princess, locked (yes, locked) in the bathroom. Mark changed out the handle several times, eventually just installing a door knob that can't be locked. As far as I know there haven't been problems down there since Princess passed almost two years ago.*

Here are some of Kodie's stories:

- *There have been multiple instances at the B&B where I have had odd things happen. It seems to me it's mainly when we begin renovations or gather new workers. I have worked at the B&B for almost 6 years now and my sister had worked there a short period before I had started. There was one time when she had the door in the room propped open with a stool from the bathroom, and while making the bed on the other side of the room, she slipped on a curtain dragging on the floor, and somehow when she fell, the stool was now next to her and she had hit her head on it.*

- *Another odd thing is doors opening and closing, hearing doors opening and closing, but nobody is there, and lights turning on and off. There have been times when Barbara and Mark would get after me for leaving the lights on, on the third floor, when I distinctly remember turning the lights off before I had left.*

- *There's also a strange knocking noise that my coworker, Connie, and I hear quite often. It's in the dining room and sounds like someone is walking or knocking on the floor above us. We even tested by asking questions and saying things like "Knock 2 times if you're a female" and such like that, to which we would get responses. Keep in mind it was only the 2 of us here. So I know I'm not going crazy!*

- *On quite a few occasions I have been cleaning in a room upstairs and heard what sounds like people laughing or talking and the stairs would be creaking slightly. I'd walk out and call for my boss and get no response. After doing that, I'd run to the next room to check the driveway and nobody was there.*

- *Also in one of the rooms (Chardonnay), there was a time when I went to get stuff from the supply closet and while walking past the doorway, I thought I saw a figure or something standing in the room in my peripheral vision, to which I quickly turned to look and*

6

at that moment it seemed to rapidly disappear, and a slight wind blew my hair and it sounded like someone whispered "Hey" in my ear. I ran downstairs so fast, and when I got to Barbara she was frantic asking me what had happened, and said I was so pale I looked like I had seen a ghost. That was the one time I was a bit creeped out. I've managed to look past everything and accept it, but there are still places in the house I don't like to go by myself (the 3rd floor, or the back of the basement). I just get an uneasy feeling.

Kodie standing on the spot where she saw the figure.

- *I'll tell you one more instance where things were strange. I was at the Inn with a different coworker about 3 years ago and it was getting late in the day, cause we had a busy schedule and we were just finishing things up when I realized my cellphone had gone missing. I knew the phone was on vibrate but still insisted that if we called it I'd find it. My phone would ring, but we couldn't hear it or find it. After about 20 minutes of looking, I decided to go back and check in all the rooms top to bottom. When I had gotten into the Cabernet room, I wound up finding my phone directly under the center of the bed flipped upside down and turned off. This wasn't the first time things had gone missing though. My sister had something similar happen to her with a TV remote she had placed on the shelf where it belonged and next thing she knew it was gone. Again, it was under the bed flipped over.*

While there didn't seem to be anything threatening or harmful, activity did appear to be consistent, and persistent. I arranged to stop by one afternoon in early April to take a look around and match the stories with their locations. (And, of course, I had to get a take-out order from my favorite vegetarian restaurant in Pine Bush, Pure City, for Bob and I.)

Kodie and Connie began my tour by heading up to the third floor. Kodie explained that they never seemed to have any problems with the queen room to the left, although while cleaning that room, they have heard someone walking in the hall.

However, something very strange, and unnerving, occurred in the twin room. Kodie and a former employee were painting the room, when suddenly the door flew open and hit the nightstand. And it repeatedly went back and forth hitting the nightstand until Kodie grabbed it and firmly closed it. Yet, a half an hour later, the door flew open again and did the same thing. When Barbara and Mark lived on the third floor in the queen room, they would often get up in the morning and find that same twin room door standing open. I examined the door knob, and it closed securely, and no amount of pulling or pushing on the door made it open.

One night a family was sleeping on the third floor—or at least trying to. The parents were in the queen room, and their son was in the twin room. In the middle of the night, the mother heard noises and a child crying in the bathroom. Assuming something was wrong with her son, she

8

rushed into the bathroom, but no one was there. Checking the twin room, she found her son sound asleep in bed.

Another family that stayed on the third floor had their teenaged son get so scared he slept with his parents. The boy swore he heard footsteps on the stairs and saw a man. Then the entire family (parents, son, and teenaged daughter) heard someone go into the bathroom, which scared them all. They were so frightened that Barbara thought they were going to have to leave, but after the initial shock, "they were cool about it, and open to the possibilities," so decided to stay, even though they experienced something unusual each of their three nights there.

The angel that watches over the very active staircase to the third floor.

There's a spa room on the third floor, as well, and both staff and guests have felt as though they were being watched. Again, it's nothing threatening in any way, just a very strong feeling that you are not alone.

Several years ago, a movie was being filmed locally, and many members of the cast and crew stayed there. Space was at a premium, so one of the assistants, Marcella, had to sleep in the spa room. In the morning, Marcella approached Kodie and said she had a question for her.

"Do weird things happen here?" Marcella asked.

She went on to describe several things that happened to her, including seeing a man sitting in a chair in the twin room. She was not the first person to see a man in that chair—perhaps a former resident of the senior home?

Does the ghost of a former resident still sit in this chair?

We descended to the second floor and went into the Champagne Room. Kodie explained that she and her sister never had anything unusual happen in that room—until they renovated the bathroom. That appeared to stir something up, and it was in this room where her sister fell onto the stool that had somehow managed to move itself across the floor. Kodie and another woman also witnessed the door to this room opening by itself.

Kodie next showed me where she was in the hallway when she saw the person standing in the Chardonnay Room. This room is directly over the dining room, and on many occasions when they were in the dining room, they have heard walking and knocking sounds over their heads, coming from this room. When this occurs, it isn't for a second or two, it is for quite a prolonged period of time. When they would go upstairs to investigate, no one would be found and the sounds stopped, but when they returned to the dining room the sounds resumed. They now attribute this to Miss Betty, a name Barbara chose to call one of the many spirits in this house, and they always address her respectfully.

Sometimes when they are working on the second floor, they will hear groups of people talking and laughing, and going up and down the stairs. Barbara joined us at this point, and she confirmed that guests most often report footsteps on the staircases when no one is there. She then introduced me to the mystery of the hollow wall.

There's a section of wall several feet long on the second floor that bows out, and when you tap on it, it's clearly hollow. Previous owners suggested to Barbara that it may have been an old laundry chute, but they were only guessing, and it would have been the largest laundry chute in existence. Mark believes it was either a closet or a dumb waiter. There didn't appear to be any chimney or pipes connected with this section of wall, so it couldn't have anything to do with a fireplace or furnace. Of course, all this mystery made me want to poke a hole and use my fiber optic camera to investigate, but as they don't have any replacement wall paper, there will be no hole-poking any time soon!

Barbara also had more information on the Champagne Room, where they had added a door and moved a wall to make a private bath. With the first round of construction, a father and son team lived on the third floor while they worked during the week. They both complained that tools kept going missing from that bathroom—never to be found. The son would often spend weekends, as well, and also complained that food he was keeping in his room went missing. It is also interesting to note, that their work proved less than adequate, as leaks made the ceiling below collapse, twice. Perhaps the spirits knew they weren't doing a good job and were trying to drive them out?

We went down to the first floor, and everyone shared their stories of hearing the footsteps and noises from the second floor while sitting or working in the dining room. Barbara also said that when she is in her living room—which is directly below the dining room—she hears footsteps and noises from above, as well. I commented that in this section of the house, whichever floor you are on, the sounds emanate from the floor above you.

There is also a hollow-sounding spot in the dining room wall, which is under the bowed out area on the second floor. So whatever this was, it extended between two floors—which only served to double my interest!

The pantry is an area where many people have commented that they get a creepy feeling. Barbara has never felt uncomfortable there, but there are some strange "thumping sounds" that are "clearly different from old house sounds," such as would be produced by settling or rattling pipes.

We next went down into Barbara's basement apartment. She showed me where her little dog had been barking furiously, and had become so frightened. We also went into a storeroom which used to be the activity room for the senior home. Kodie admitted she doesn't like any part of the basement, and in the former activity room I had to agree with her. I felt uncomfortable, and I also felt like we had company; perhaps more than one unseen visitor.

There are several reasons Kodie doesn't like the basement. For starters, she saw a shadow figure in a doorway. Also, she spent a few nights when Barbara and Mark were away, and she could hear footsteps above her on the first floor "all night long." One night the sound "was distinct, like someone in boots walked across the floor." She had her sister spend the following night with her so she didn't have to be alone.

Mark has also heard the footsteps, and on several occasions was convinced someone had broken into the house. He would run upstairs and search everywhere, but never found anyone. Still, he believes it all has a rational explanation.

We toured the yard and looked at the additions from the outside only, as there are currently tenants. There is also a cottage being renovated, and a former tenant often told Barbara that someone was in the basement, which had an outside door. She would hear that door open and close, and hear people moving around the basement. However, when Barbara would come and investigate, she always found the door securely locked, so no one could have entered. However, this woman was adamant about what she heard.

At this point, I had certainly heard enough compelling stories to want to return. I contacted psychic Barbara Roth Bleitzhofer and just five days later, we were at the Pine Bush House—after dinner at Pure City, of course. After all the introductions, I mentioned that Barb B. had already told me some things she had sensed about the house just by driving by over the years.

"Really? You've driven by this place before?" Barbara G. asked, her curiosity already piqued. "Well, you sit right down! And don't sugar coat it; spit it right out."

"The first thing is, there are children, and they like to play," Barb began. "And they do like to hide things."

We all immediately thought of the missing TV remotes, cell phone, tools, and food. Also, when Barb said the words "hide things," the K2 EMF meter lit up. Nothing like hitting a bull's eye in the first minute of an investigation!

Barb, Connie, Barbara G., and Kodie in the lovely dining room
at the start of our investigation.

Barb went on to ask who died of a heart attack. Of course, with its long history of families and as a senior home, there could be a long list of heart attack victims. Barb was unaware that this had been a senior home, and for now, we wanted to keep it that way so as not to influence her, so we just said we didn't know who that could have been.

She also talked about the presence of an older woman, a middle-aged woman, and several other women, so the roster of spirits was already growing in leaps and bounds. She saw this group of women in white aprons (at which point the K2 lit up again), cooking, and caring for people.

Speaking more about the children, who she said can be heard running around, Barb specifically described a boy with a "newspaper boy-type cap," short pants, a "poofed-out shirt," and a vest; an "early 1900s look." When I asked if he passed away on the property, she replied that he had, and "it was something with a horse," and said there must have been stables nearby. She also talked about a little girl who died "of fever."

The K2 meter once again went off when Barb started talking about "the strong smell of apples." This was something she had smelled by just looking at a picture of the house, and now it was even more pronounced. Of course, this was just something Barb could detect with her sixth sense, as no one else smelled anything. At the time, we didn't know what significance this had, but weeks later when I was conducting some research on the area, I discovered that there used to be a distillery right behind the house. The owner would pay local boys to collect apples around town, which he turned into hard cider. I'll bet that produced a *very* strong smell of apples!

After the initial impressions, we decided to go through the house, but we didn't get far. Barb was immediately drawn to the beautiful, old, Decker piano in the parlor. She saw an African-American jazz/ragtime pianist attached to his beloved piano, and saw that he had made a lot of money playing it in some type of roadhouse. He would put his cap on top of the piano for tips from his appreciative audiences, and this practice also earned him the nickname Cappy. Barbara G. said that while the piano was made in New York, they purchased it from a man in California who had converted it to a player piano. Its history prior to the California owner was not known, but it was certainly old enough for the jazz era.

I asked if Cappy could give us a sign, and my K2 meter lit up like a Christmas tree. A wave of goose bumps swept over all of us. These are the type of moments that kept me ghost hunting!

Barb at "Cappy's" piano.

Barb was next drawn to the Victrola, where there was "a very intense energy" and she could hear "the old tenors singing, like Caruso." There was a male energy attached to it, and he "could be very sharp-tempered." The yellow light on the K2 illuminated when she said that, and a moment later we heard a *thud* from upstairs.

"Is anyone upstairs?" I asked.

"No," Barbara G. replied, but then added, "At least not any paying customers."

We went upstairs to the Cabernet Room were Barb felt an elderly woman "with severe respiratory problems" who passed away in that room. Barbara G. asked if she was getting a name, and Barb quickly replied, "Betsey or Betty." In the Zinfandel Suite, Barb again brought up the name, this time refining it to Betty Ann, and saying that the woman would have liked this room. Was this the Miss Betty that everyone addressed with respect? At the very least, it was quite a coincidence!

15

This Zinfandel Suite was one that Barb felt had a wonderful "honeymoon suite" vibe to it, and it was probably the one room in the house where no one had experienced anything unusual. The only other thing Barb sensed here was the spirit of a large, male, gray and white cat who still likes to "curl up by the fireplace." We speculated that he might be one of the reasons the dogs bark!

Next was the Chardonnay Room, where Barb believed "the master" of the house lived. She even began coughing from the heavy pipe tobacco smoke she sensed in this room, and she kept hearing the name Troy. Barb then asked me if I had a specific question about this room—actually, she *told* me I had a question—and I asked her to put her hands on the wall over the hollow area. She felt there were secrets surrounding something in the wall, and kept hearing the name Henry.

"There was also a birth in this room, and a whole lot of yelling going on," Barb continued. "There was also a lot of talking, and meetings in this room. If there is something inside this wall, it has to do with all this, with communications. There may be papers in there. It's like a hunt; like an Easter egg hunt. They're saying, 'Go ahead, find it.' "

"So there is some secret to be uncovered?" I asked.

"Yes, it's like a hunt," Barb responded.

Barbara G. asked Barb to feel the other side of the wall, in the hallway, and when she placed her hands on that section of wall she actually gasped.

"There's three. And someone is walking over here," Barb said, deeply engrossed and shaken by the intensity of the experience.

My K2 meter also lit up at that moment and the air turned icy cold.

"Three what?" I asked. "Three spirits?"

"Three lines of stuff going through. It's like they walled up the three things. One, two, three, I keep seeing that over and over. And it happened during the winter months. Why is there such a huge gap between here and the other side of the wall?"

"We don't know," Barbara G. replied.

"This side…" Barb began, and then hesitated before continuing. "This side, I'm just going to say it. This side is scarier. I'm getting the three clusters and then the lines, because the lines were drawn."

"Now what does that mean?" Babara G. asked.

"You know, I'm not sure why…what 'lines were drawn' would mean."

"The only thing I can think of," I chimed in, "was that they had to make some sort of decision…and it wasn't good for someone."

"No, it wasn't," Barb agreed. "You know, one of the maids was a snoop."

We all just looked at one another as Barb suddenly changed gears, and I saw the look of concern on Kodie's and Connie's faces.

"You mean in the *past*?" I asked for clarification.

"Oh no, no, no, I didn't mean either of you!" Barb said, pointing at Kodie and Connie, as we all started laughing.

Barb explained that long ago there was a maid who "snooped around" and she was somehow connected with what was hidden inside the wall. She still snoops around to this day, looking for something, and she is one of the spirits that goes up and down the staircases. As Barb spoke, the meter was going off like crazy and we all had the chills.

What secrets are hidden between these walls? What were the circumstances of the birth, and why was so much time and energy put into talking about it and deciding what was to be done? What is it that the maid continues to look for to this day? The writer in me wants to imagine all manner of sinister scenarios, but the investigator can only state that there is an unusual structure that appears hollow. Until I can get a fiber optic camera in the walls, or they decide upon some major renovations, this mystery will continue.

Next was the Champagne Room, which felt particularly cold.

"There's a lot of movement in here," Barb began. "This is one of the most active places. It was a woman's room and this was her sanctuary, and she just wants everyone to get out! Her only rest and relaxation time was in this room. And they are saying the name Rosemarie. She was like a nanny or an aunt who came to help out, and she gets frazzled. She doesn't like kids; they are to be seen and not heard."

Barb hesitated to go into the bathroom and said she did not want to cross the threshold. When she finally did, she let out a distinctive moaning/groaning sound that I knew meant she was encountering something very unpleasant. She felt that long ago, this was a closet or small room used for punishment, perhaps locking children in here, in the dark.

"This isn't a happy bathroom!" she concluded, but then tried to soften her pronouncement, but only a bit. "But it's a beautiful bathroom...but I wouldn't want to spend any time in here."

The third floor was next, and Barb immediately felt "like they definitely all hang out up here. This is not the children, this is the adults."

"So this is the most active part of the house?" I asked.

"Yes, and they're serious. They're not harmful, but when you get scared, they get a kick out of it."

The predominant energies were of a couple—a "very rough, angry man" who was abusive to his "weak" wife.

"There is also a very elderly man who just hangs out—you know, the 'I'm just going to die here' feeling. I have to tell you, the energy in here makes me nervous [in the queen bedroom]. I couldn't sleep in this room. It's just intense energy."

She also got the unpleasant image of someone hanging or shooting themselves in the 1930s, possibly in the closet. Everyone agreed they don't like that closet. There may also have been a fire long ago, possibly involving the old gas lines, which still exist throughout the house. Barb also felt like "an old-time pickpocket once lived here" and still takes various objects.

In the single bedroom, Barb encountered a "lot of talking and scheming," as well as a confused old man who may have been suffering from dementia. He "wondered why he had been put here." At this point, I was ready to tell Barb the history of the house, but she beat me to it.

"It's like this was some kind of a nursing home," she said, which of course, made me smile. I knew she could do it!

Barbara G. and I confirmed that fact and filled her in on the details. I also told Barb that the chair in which she was sitting was where people had seen an elderly man—perhaps he was the man with dementia, and he is still confused even after death? Many of the pieces fell into place now, from the women in the aprons, to the variety of elderly spirits she had sensed.

There were more unpleasant feelings in the bathroom and adjoining storage area, where people may have been kept as a form of discipline or punishment. Barb felt there had been some abuse of the elderly residents, and at the very least, severe neglect. The spa room was also intense, but of a much better nature.

I wondered how the mysterious bowed-out section of wall on the second floor corresponded to the third floor, so I went down to knock on the wall so we could find out. As everyone else remained on the third floor, I went down the staircase and started banging on the wall. It turned out that the bathroom shower was over the bowed-out area, but I paid a price for that information.

As I knocked with my right hand, the EMF meter in my left hand lit up to the red light—the strongest reading. At the same instant, I got a powerful electric jolt in my right hand, as if I had stuck my finger in a socket! I jumped back and just looked at my hand and the wall for a few seconds, trying to figure out what just happened. Apparently, someone was not happy that I was banging on that wall—which made me want to do it even more, but one shock was enough. I admit it, it freaked me out!

We went back to the dining room and looked at an early 1900s postcard of the house. One thing I noticed right away was that there were two chimneys, one on the left side outer wall, and one on the back wall. There were no chimneys in the center of the house, so the bowed-out area had definitely not been a fireplace.

Next came the basement. Barb said she sensed a very sad feeling in the rec room, and didn't want to stay in there. She saw "either a very short woman, or a woman in a wheelchair" in that room.

"No one really had any fun down here," she said. "There were a lot of miserable people. And some nasty ones, too."

As I asked if there was something we could do to help them move on, the K2 meter lit up to yellow. Barb talked about some ways to use candles, smudging, and various scents to help lighten the atmosphere throughout the house, as well as how to speak to the spirits to encourage them to move on.

We went outside and looked at the two-story addition that used to be the dormitory section of the senior home. Barb did not get good vibes from the structure; reinforcing her belief that residents were not always treated well. She also encountered that same strong smell of apples, and was adamant that something in the past in this area had once produced that smell, which as I mentioned, I discovered was true.

I thought we were winding down the investigation at this point, but as we stepped onto the front porch and were about to go back in the house, *the front door swung open on its own!* I took that to mean that either we were now welcome, or the invisible inhabitants had more in store for us. It turned out to be the latter.

We went back to the dining room to discuss everything, and in less than two minutes there was some loud banging upstairs. Despite the electric shock I had received on the second floor, I headed for the staircase. Standing in the middle of the staircase—so I could still talk with everyone, but also hear what was happening on the second floor—the combination of footsteps and banging was clear and obvious.

"Are you kidding me?" I said in amazement, and partial disbelief, at the blatant activity.

I ran back and grabbed my digital recorder, and when I returned to the stairs I asked for a sign.

Bang!

Immediately, right above me was a loud sound that was captured on the recording. That was followed by distinct footsteps.

"Is that you?" Connie asked me from the dining room.

"That is *not* me," I assured her. "Somebody is walking around. Seriously, nobody is moving?"

"I don't even think I'm breathing!" Barbara G. replied.

Connie then asked whoever it was to take three steps. I couldn't hear the response from where I was standing, but everyone else in the dining room heard three, quick, knocking sounds above them. Barb felt it was an elderly man who used to bang his cane on the floor to get someone's attention. The sounds then increased to a level where I could hear them again, and I was so impressed, I couldn't help but say, "Wow!"

The remarkable noises continued for a few more moments, but then stopped. I remained on the stairs for several more minutes, and we asked some more questions, but apparently the paranormal demonstration was over. I have been ghost hunting for a long time, and those sounds were among the most "in your face" experiences that I've ever had.

We spent some time talking about Miss Betty, the children, and all the other personalities that make this place so fascinating. Then Barb couldn't resist bringing up some personal messages she had been getting for the living members of our group that night. I don't reveal such information, but rest assured she was, as always, on target.

Barb concluded by affirming that for all the activity at Pine Bush House, there was nothing threatening and nothing that would ever hurt anyone. She was also clear that since Barbara and Mark have owned the property, the atmosphere in the house has improved dramatically. They have brought joy and caring into the place, which are powerful forces capable of dispelling any darkness from the past.

For now, though, it appears that many spirits still choose to remain—either because this was the home they loved, or perhaps because they were confused at the time of their death and don't know to move on. Whatever the reasons, Pine Bush House provides a unique opportunity to enjoy the wonderful hospitality and décor, as well as experience another world that few have glimpsed—a world we will all ultimately enter. But that doesn't mean we won't be able to come back to visit...

I stood in the middle of this staircase and clearly heard
footsteps and banging sounds.

Butterfly Kisses
Hastings-on-Hudson, NY

In early November of 2013, "Susan's" mother passed away. The burial was to take place at the Mt. Hope cemetery in Hastings-on-Hudson, New York, on November 4th. Susan's father was also buried there, but she had never been to the gravesite. At the time her father passed away in 1982, Susan was pregnant and it was decided that it would be too stressful for her to attend the services.

So when she arrived at the cemetery, it was the first time Susan and her family saw her father's grave. She bent over so she could brush the headstone to clean it, and then took her place by her mother's casket as the service was about to begin. While she stood there, "suddenly the clouds parted and this bright beam of sunlight hit me in the eyes." It was so bright it made her eyes water and she had to close them. When she opened her eyes again, she saw that there was now a rock sitting on top of the headstone!

In addition to the priest, there were only six other people at the service—none of whom was standing near her father's headstone, which was one grave away from her mother's, as her grandmother was buried in between. As no one was within arm's reach, she couldn't understand how the rock had gotten there.

As soon as the service concluded, Susan went to examine the rock. It was irregularly shaped—"just like any rock you would find on the ground"—but it looked to be made of the same type of stone as the headstone. Carved on the rock were two things—a butterfly, and the words "Miss You." A warm feeling flooded her body, and she immediately thought of her father. When she was a little girl, he would brush his eyelashes across her cheek and tell her they were butterfly kisses.

Susan told her husband she wanted to keep the rock, but then decided she should leave it there. She was the last person to leave the gravesite, and when she got back to the car she changed her mind and wanted to go back and get the rock. But when she returned to the gravesite, the rock on the headstone was gone!

The family has no explanation for this mysterious rock. They all saw that it was definitely *not* there when they first arrived, and then it appeared when no one was standing near enough to place it there. Then the butterfly rock disappeared when no one was even standing in the cemetery!

About a week later, Susan returned to the cemetery and guess what was waiting for her at her father's grave? There was the butterfly rock sitting on the headstone again!

"I said, 'Look, dad, I appreciate you leaving me this message, but you can stop now,' " Susan said out loud. As much as she loved her dad, this was getting on her nerves!

Once again, she left the rock, but this time she took a picture of it.

Who carved this stone? Who placed it on the headstone? How was it able to appear and disappear? Maybe someday when you are visiting the gravesite of a loved one, you will also be lucky enough to get a message from the other side.

Athelhampton House

If anyone had told me that I would someday be writing about the ghost of an ape that belonged to one of my 15th century English ancestors, I would have called them crazy. Yet here I am today, about to do just that. But let me back up a bit and first explain how this all came about.

I have spent decades researching the history of events and people, often tracing back family lines for generations. I knew more about men and women I had never met, and with whom I had no connection, than I did about my own family. Then one fateful day in early 2014, I decided to "spend a little time" on a few genealogy websites to see if I could find out anything about my own history.

Well, literally hundreds of hours later, I have amassed a family tree which currently contains 2,035 individuals, stretches back well over a thousand years, and includes everyone from simple farmers and carpenters, to adventurers, pioneers, soldiers, knights, and kings and queens from over a dozen different countries. I always become completely obsessed in all of my research projects, and when I finally focused my attention on researching my own family, I became hopelessly addicted. I think my husband was ready to set up an intervention.

How marvelous it was, though, to discover that I carried the DNA of people who were among the first Europeans to come to the New World, and had helped in the founding of towns throughout New England, such as Cambridge, Massachusetts, and Hartford, Connecticut. I discovered two towns in Canada which were actually named after my ancestors, who literally cut their homes and farms out of the wilderness. And I traced these people back to their families in Great Britain--families which stretched as far as the Norman Conquest; even back to France, and then to their early Viking roots.

Along this incredible journey, I found the Martin family, who proudly traced their lineage back to Sir William Martyn (1460-1503). Sir William was a wealthy ship owner, a member of parliament, and had served as Lord Mayor of London in 1492. His most enduring legacy, however, is the magnificent Athelhampton House in Dorchester, England, which was built in 1485.

If you don't plan on visiting England anytime soon, you can see the house in the 1972 film, *Sleuth*, on the *Doctor Who* episode *The Seeds of Doom*, or in the 2009 film, *From Time to Time*. It was also one of the first places investigated for the popular British television show *Most Haunted*. In fact, the title of that TV show is quite appropriate, as Athelhampton House has often been called one of the most haunted places in England, which is saying a lot, considering you can't toss a crumpet there without hitting a place that has ghosts.

While no one can say for certain it *is* one of England's most haunted places, I think few would argue that it certainly has one of the most unique ghosts on record. Somewhere along the way, Sir William acquired an ape for a pet, and the two became very attached to one another. This is evident in that there is not only a stained glass window of the ape at Athelhampton House, but Sir William had his beloved pet carved into his tomb effigy in Puddletown Church, where it obediently sits at his feet for all eternity.

Unfortunately, while Sir William was away on business and the house was undergoing some construction, the pet ape was accidentally sealed up behind a wall, where it died of starvation. However, for hundreds of years, residents and guests have claimed to hear the ghost of the poor ape scratching on the walls, still trying to get out!

Of course, the minute I read this, and realized I was related to a man who had an ape ghost in a beautiful English manor house, I had to contact the place. I explained that I was a descendant of Sir William, and that I wrote the *Ghost Investigator* series, and was delighted to receive the following reply from the owner:

Dear Linda

Thank you for your message. We get lots of descendants contacting us, people are fascinated by their family trees and it's always wonderful to discover someone who has left their mark upon history. There are some wonderful newly restored effigies of the family in Puddletown Church, there should be pictures of them on our Face book page.

Athelhampton has a wealth of ghost stories connected with the House, some are dubious but others have remained with the building for generations. The Ape is the principle story and the most unusual. He is featured in a stain glass window in The Great Chamber and we also have an Ape Gargoyle above the front door, which had his missing head replaced by a local stone mason 12 years ago.

Any ancient building will conjure imaginings in one's mind, therefore the 'power of suggestion' cannot be discounted. However many people working, visiting, and as in my case, living here, have had so many vivid

experiences, I would say that it is beyond doubt that Athelhampton has layer upon layer of some sort of residual activity.

Our two children have witnessed figures, day and night, we have had furniture move - look on You Tube for Athelhampton TV, 'Most Haunted' episode covers a lot of our stories but frustratingly did not catch on camera the cot rocking, only the sound - But I saw it.

We have had some problems, as well. Our private bedrooms and the corridor accessing them, which are not open to the public, have had very 'busy' periods which affected our sleep and general sense of wellbeing. Figures walking into bedrooms at night. Doors being banged, the strong smell of stale cigarettes. A very strong sense of being watched and followed.

The most recent sighting was just before Christmas. We have a lady who cleans the bedroom area once a week, she has worked for us for a number of years. Her other clients own old buildings, but up until now, she has never experienced anything. Within the space of 10 minutes, she saw a dark, hooded figure, directly in front of her and moving very swiftly through the corridor, and then again, up the spiral staircase and through my son's bathroom. She was very excited as you can imagine!

In my experience, people share their ghost stories rather timidly, feeling perhaps that they have more to lose than to gain, fearing a taint of madness. They are usually otherwise sensible people, not given to fancy or superstition and very often are sceptics themselves until they witness something.

I hope this is of some use. If you need more stories I can relay them to you. I have tried to give you a rough idea.

Yours
Andrea Cooke

After reading this, I had to use all my willpower to restrain myself from booking the next flight to London! Dark, hooded figures walking about, in addition to an ape ghost! But as I was to discover, there are even more spirits:

- One day a woman was in the Great Hall (photo below) reading a book, when two men came crashing through the door, engaged in a fierce sword fight. They fought until one of the combatants was wounded in his arm, and then both men left the room. When the woman told the owner about the duel, she discovered that everyone was having tea at the time, and no one fitting either of her descriptions of the two men was in the house. It is suspected that she had glimpsed a scene from back in the days of the English Civil War.

- Many people over the years have seen an apparition they call the "Grey Lady" walking throughout the house. A former owner often saw her actually passing through walls!
- There are tapping sounds in the wine cellar that have been attributed to a cooper hammering his barrels.

Sir William's effigy in Puddletown Church, with his faithful ape at his feet.

The crest in each case is the chained ape. The family motto was "he who looks at Martyn's ape, Martyn's ape shall look at him". At the very top of the first window is a celestial monkey with angel's wings. He gazes bird-like into a gilded mirror that shows his reflection in its glass. The ape, which now wears a Saxon crown and carries a mace, is the heraldic badge of the Cooke family.

A clip from Athelhampton House's guide book showing the stained glass with the ape, and mentioning the bizarre family motto.

The list of paranormal activity goes on. But, suffice it to say, Athelhampton House makes my Top Ten list of Ye Olde Haunted Places, and to think that my ancestors are to be thanked for it all! No wonder I'm the Ghost Investigator; it's in my genes!

The famous pyramid shrubbery in one of the estate's many gardens. What other ghosts walk these ancient grounds?

Par(anormal) for the Course
Congers, NY

I suppose after a few hundred haunted sites I shouldn't be surprised by anything, but there's still an occasional case that raises an eyebrow. Last year when I investigated the old Garnerville factories with Hallie and Gary, he told me that some weird things happened where he worked—at a golf course!

One wouldn't imagine the beautifully manicured greens and fancy clubhouses of golf courses to be places where lost souls would wander, but consider these startling facts:

- Over 3,000 golfers die every year, and that statistic is just for U.S. golf courses
- Because of their remote locations—and the often advanced ages of the golfers—heart attacks on golf courses are 95% fatal
- From 1990 to 2006, there were 147,700 golf cart injuries in the U.S.
- Since 1975, dozens of golfers have been killed by lightning
- People have been killed and severely injured by getting hit in the head by golf balls

- Frustrated golfers have used their clubs to beat to death other golfers. Several angry golfers have also accidentally killed themselves by smashing their clubs and having splinters of the shafts pierce their arteries.
- One man threw his golf bag and clubs in a pond, and then realized his car keys were in the bag. When he jumped in the pond to retrieve the keys, he drowned.

The purpose of presenting this information is not to make you run screaming at the sight of a golf course, but to make you aware that looks can be deceiving. Any place can be haunted. And let's not forget the ever-present paranormal danger for sites with sprawling properties—what tragedies occurred on that land in the past?

With all this I mind, I present Rockland Lake Championship Golf Course in Congers, New York, where in recent years there have been several deaths from heart attacks, with a total of at least 23 deaths just since the 1990s. And as the golf course began construction in the 1960s, that number is most likely considerably higher; at least double. When I first heard this, my initial thought was that there are some battlefields that haven't seen that many deaths!

I had hoped to have a clear night to check out the golf course, as well as the clubhouse, so naturally it was pouring rain the night in March that my husband, Bob, and I picked up Hallie and Gary and headed toward Rockland Lake. Of course, with the horrendous winter we had just endured, we were thankful it wasn't snow!

As we approached a cemetery that's along the road, close to the golf course entrance (there are actually *two* cemeteries bordering the property), we all heard what at first sounded like a distant car alarm. I took a quick look around for the car making all the noise, but didn't see anything. At first, I really didn't think anything of it, until a few seconds later I realized the sound level was not changing, and it should have been either getting louder or fainter, depending upon whether we were moving closer to, or farther away, from the car alarm.

Then Hallie said, "It's coming from inside the car."

Bob and I looked at each other and couldn't think of what would be inside the van that would be making such a noise. My gear bag was on the floor behind my seat, so I spun around, leaned down, and sure enough, *the alarm was inside of my gear bag*! In a what-the-hell moment, I grabbed the bag and opened the side pocket where I kept my motion detector, and sure enough it was wailing away. I shut it off, but couldn't imagine how this had happened.

The day before, I had installed a new battery and tested the motion detector. I then turned it off and put it in my bag. Had I not turned it off, the alarm would have gone off and kept on going. It is also not an easy switch to slide on and off, and it certainly couldn't happen by just sitting in my bag. How it turned itself on at that moment is a complete mystery, but it got my attention and I said to myself, "Game on!"

Waiting for us at the clubhouse were employees Susan, Kerri, and Alice, and we began our evening by hearing their stories. Susan has worked there since 2008, and had no prior knowledge of any spooky occurrences when she started the job. However, she was quickly suspicious when in her first month of employment, she was all alone and heard a "very, very loud" banging sound in her boss' office next door. It sounded like a heavy, metal pipe falling to the floor. Unlocking the door, she looked inside to see what had fallen, and nothing was out of place. Also, I noticed that the floor was carpeted, which would had deadened such a sound if a metal pipe had actually struck the floor.

This had occurred in daylight, so this is not a place where things only go bump in the night. Susan also explained that when she arrives early in the morning, the place feels particularly creepy—a sentiment that Gary and the others confirmed. Gary went on to say that he is often there at night at closing, and there is a strong sense of uneasiness in the clubhouse, even though visually there doesn't seem to be anything creepy about the relatively new building.

Alice then mentioned some trouble they have all had in their office.

"Oh yeah," Susan chimed in, "The Black Hole."

"The Black Hole?" I asked, laughing.

"We call it that because things always disappear," Susan said. "And doors somehow lock themselves. It happens so often we always make sure we check the locks before closing a door, and few minutes later we come back and door is locked."

Alice explained how the same thing happens to the safe. They will open it, and even though no one goes near it, it locks itself and they constantly have to re-enter the combination. After hearing about the locks, all the papers and objects that go missing, and the strange sounds they hear, I realized they had good reason to call their office The Black Hole!

Another thing that often happens is that they will see lights inside the clubhouse when it is closed and empty—lights that, on their own, go off as inexplicably as they turn on. Alice and Susan were driving up to the building one night, and through the trees they could see that there was a light on in the building. Alice assumed someone had left the light on the previous day, but when they pulled up in front of the clubhouse, the place was completely dark.

Gary has often seen a light on in one of the attics of the building, where "no one ever goes," but when he went inside to investigate the source, the light was off. Susan said that two other employees had also seen a light on in the attic. She then explained that there weren't any switches on the main floor to operate those lights. In order to turn on a light in one of the attics, you have to set up a tall ladder, open the access panel, climb into the attic and pull the string to turn on the light. And when the place is locked and empty, that's quite a feat!

I asked what had been on the grounds before the current clubhouse. There had been the original clubhouse, but no one knew what it looked like. Going way back, the area was farm land in the former town of

Rockland Lake. It would take some research to find out if any houses or other buildings once stood on this site.

The attic where the light goes on and off by itself.
(And those are not orbs, it was raining!)

Kerri then talked about her most interesting encounter. She was in the office with Susan, and they were settling the accounts of the day when Kerri felt a little shove on her shoulder. She assumed Susan was trying to get her attention—although why she would choose to push her shoulder she couldn't imagine—but when she turned to see what Susan wanted, she saw that Susan was on the other side of a tall desk, well out of reach.

"Did you just touch me?" Kerri asked Susan. But, of course, Susan had no idea what Kerri was talking about.

By phone, I also interviewed Peggy that night, who has worked there since 2007. On two different occasions, she has heard her name being called when she was alone in the building. Peggy and another employee have also seen a figure in various parts of the building, and assumed it was one another—until they discovered that the other person was nowhere near where the figure was seen walking or sitting. This most often happens early in the morning.

When I asked Peggy about any unusual smells, she replied that there is sometimes a very strong scent of carnations.

"And I hate carnations. I literally *hate* carnations," she emphasized. "I can't take the smell of them. They remind me of a wake and it freaked me out when I've smelled them between my office and the pro shop."

As Peggy was speaking about carnations reminding her of a wake, we heard a loud thudding sound coming from inside the men's room!

Peggy then recalled her own incident with a light on in the attic, but the incident went far beyond a mere light. It was 4:30am, and she and another employee were walking toward the building. There was a light on in the attic, and Peggy could swear she saw a figure silhouetted in the attic window!

As I was wrapping up the interviews, we were joined by Hallie's friend, Bob, who we called "Bob 2," to differentiate him from my husband, Bob. We decided to start our paranormal stakeout in the hallway where the restrooms are located. Both male and female employees have heard noises, such as doors opening and closing in the restrooms at times when no one else was present. In fact, the entrance door to the ladies' room makes a very distinctive grinding/groaning sound that can't be mistaken for anything else, and that sound has been clearly heard by people who thought they were all alone.

I chose to sit on the floor at the end of the hallway, with my back to a door. The restrooms were down the hall a short distance to my left. I sat down and started getting my equipment out of my gear bag. Suddenly, the door handle behind me started rattling, and the entire door shook as though someone was violently trying to open it. I assumed another member of the staff was joining us, and as I didn't want someone to trample my gear (or me!), I scooped up my equipment and gear bag in my arms and pushed myself out of the way.

I sat there for a few seconds looking at the door, waiting for whoever it was to come in, but it suddenly stopped rattling and fell silent. The door was apparently locked, but I didn't hear anyone walking away, or any sounds of any kind. I turned to the group behind me who were just settling down onto the floor along the walls at the other end of the hall.

"Are you expecting someone else?" I asked, still clutching all my gear in my arms. "Someone was just trying to get in here."

I was shocked to find out that the door didn't lead to the outside, or even another section of the building. It was, in fact, a locked closet door, and no one was inside! I took a moment to process that information and try to rationalize it with what I just witnessed. We did test openings and closings with the restroom doors to see if changes in air pressure could make the closet door rattle so vigorously, but they had absolutely no effect. I moved around the hall, stomping and bouncing on the floor to see if that made the closet door move, but it did nothing.

I could only conclude that one of the spirits here was messing with me, as it happened just after I sat down and started getting ready for the investigation. Of course, I didn't have anything set up yet, so I didn't get any video or photos. And I didn't even think to record the sounds on my digital recorder, because I honestly didn't think anything strange was happening. I just thought someone else was joining us. It turns out I was right, only it wasn't a living person who joined us!

Once I got the cameras and meters set up and everyone was seated, I asked if anyone wanted to give us a sign or make a sound. Immediately there was a banging noise at the other end of the hall.

"That was a sound," I stated for the recorder, and then got confirmation that everyone else heard

I took this infrared photo of the closet door, unfortunately right *after* it was rattling.

it, as well. They felt it had originated in the long room behind them. "Are you a golfer who died here?"

Tense seconds ticked by as we waited breathlessly in the darkness, until Gary's cell phone rang loudly. I exclaimed a choice word as we all practically jumped out of our skins. It was Peggy returning Gary's call, and it was at this point that I interviewed her over the speaker phone.

An infrared image of our group in the hallway.

We heard a few more odd sounds, and the infrared camcorder went completely out of focus a couple of times, which usually only happens when something passes close in front of the camera lens. Nothing was moving, though—as far as we could see. Bob also had the K2 meter light up briefly in the doorway between the hallway and the adjoining room, where we had earlier heard the sound. Hallie and a few of the others also felt a cold breeze pass by their faces, and no windows or doors were open to the outside.

We then all moved to the tables and chairs in the next room. Soon after we settled down, there were footsteps from the adjoining main entrance room. Our group was all accounted for, so it wasn't any of us. I asked if it was a woman, with no response. I asked if it was a man, and still there was silence. However, when Hallie asked if this person died here, there was a banging noise above us, loud enough to be recorded. That was followed a short time later by a voice, but none of us could determine what the voice said, or whether it was male or female.

I asked if there was someone connected with the old building, with no response. Then just as I was about to ask if someone was connected with the cemetery, there was the creepiest, most skin-crawling moaning! We all heard it, but none of us could tell where it came from.

"What the hell?" I asked, as the spooky cry even gave me goose bumps. I realized we had just taken a step into another level of haunted with that disturbing moaning. I decided to call Barb to see if she could shed some light on this place, even from a distance.

I got her on the phone at her home, where she was in the middle of watching *Ghost Adventures,* and only told her that I was at a "haunted location and some things have been happening." She immediately said that she felt "tightness, pressure, and a nervous feeling." I confirmed that some nerves were getting frayed! Barb also felt as if someone was choking and having trouble breathing, and that there had been some deaths at our location. She believed that a man had been attacked by a person or persons who came up behind him.

"Where the hell are you?" she asked, feeling the intensity of the place.

I still didn't tell her where we were, but I did tell her about the door rattling behind me, and of the sounds we were hearing. She reiterated the feeling of an attack that resulted in "one hell of a fight," with some injuries, possibly a death. Had murder left its imprint here?

"How am I supposed to work here after hearing that?" Gary asked, as he listened to Barb's information.

Barb then asked if there was a lake nearby, and of course, there is the large Rockland Lake, as well as a small pond on the golf course. She saw the brutal attack happening "back when it was all farm land" and believed it could have been around 1840. One the one hand, it was reasonably good news that this wasn't anything that happened recently, but on the other hand, it was quite disturbing to hear that distant events on the property were still having repercussions today.

When I finally told her we were at a golf course, Barb immediately said that there had been recent deaths there, and some of those spirits still walked around the greens. Barb also told me that the name Patterson kept coming up, so it was something for us to look for. We searched all over to see if something was obvious, and only found the Patterson, New Jersey golf course listed on a big map, which didn't really seem to have any significance.

As we were all curious about the activity with the safe closing and locking by itself, I simply asked Barb if she picked up anything regarding a safe. She said that the man who used to handle the accounts is still attached to the safe, and "doesn't trust anyone" so "he will close and lock" it quite frequently!

Our next stop on the stakeout was the main central room. We all asked a variety of questions, but while there were some noises from around the building, we didn't get anything definitive, so we decided to move onto "The Black Hole," where things were decidedly different.

The central room and lunch counter.

We were all filing into the offices when someone brushed against Alice. At first, she thought it was Bob 2 walking past her, but then she saw that he was on the other side of the room. Turning around to see who it had been, she found that no one was there! She was certain that someone had physically brushed up against her, so it was quite startling to find out that nothing physical had done it.

A few moments later, I got a chill and was covered in goose bumps. The energy level had ratcheted up a few notches and almost everyone was feeling something unusual, and uneasy.

"Okay, this is the real deal here," I said, as I took a seat on the floor and prepared for more unsettling activity, which occurred within minutes with a loud noise right behind me. There was also some sort of tapping in the next room. We sat quietly for several minutes, and I was beginning to think that the little flurry of activity was over, when one the ladies suddenly gasped in surprise.

The door to the hallway was closed and there was no one else in the building besides us, but the door rattled as if someone wanted to come into the offices. This is exactly what I had experienced with the closet door on the other side of the building. I went over to the door and asked if someone was in the hallway. In response there was a deep *thud* as if something heavy hit the floor just on the other side of the door.

"What the hell?" I said, taking a step back. "I don't feel like there's anything good out there, and I really don't like it."

I actually took another step back, and said that if anyone else wanted to stand by the door, that was fine by me. Bob took the K2 meter by the door, and it did have some lights flash a few times, but the bombshell hit when Hallie asked if this is where the murder occurred. An icy chill swept through us and the meter lit up all the way to the red light. It was an intense, unnerving moment that shook us all. Had this building been placed on the site of an old murder? Just for confirmation, I asked again if the murder occurred in the doorway, and in an immediate response, the meter lit up again.

We asked a few more questions but the meter didn't respond and there was silence, until Gary asked if the murder victim was buried on the property. A couple of lights flickered, but it wasn't definitive.

"You are buried on this property?" I asked again. "You are going to have to make it light up so we—"

41

I never got to finish my sentence because the meter lit all the way up to red again! Everyone gasped or let out a startled yell. Listening to the audio later it was like the sound track to a horror movie during a shocking scene. It was such a clear and immediate response—you can't make up this stuff! I may not have put it very eloquently, but I summed up our experience by saying, "That was a 'Holy Shit!' moment."

I could have left it at that, but I recalled what Barb had said, and asked, "Was your name Patterson?"

Right on cue the meter lit up again!

"You're solving the mystery!" Hallie exclaimed.

Barb actually solved the mystery; I just obtained the visual confirmation.

"I will tell your story," I continued. "Will it help you if I do?"

As soon as I spoke, there was a banging noise right above our heads in the attic. Either there were some very big mice, or I had just gotten another direct response. We asked several other questions but nothing else happened, and it appeared that the intense flurry of activity was over in The Black Hole.

At this point, we found out that when Bob 2 drove up to the club house, he saw a light on in the attic. There was no reason for him to think this was anything unusual, so he hadn't mentioned it before. We all ran outside to see if the light was still on, but it was off. Again, the only way this light can be turned on is if someone climbs a ladder to the access door, goes into the attic and switches it on, which of course, none of us had done. But obviously, something was in the attic that night, messing with the light.

Our next stop was the kitchen, but there were so many noisy appliances running that the digital recorder and EMF meter were useless, and we practically had to shout to hear one another. However, our own sixth senses were telling us that this was not a good or happy place. I felt very much on edge and my attention was continually drawn to a doorway, as if I expected someone to walk in. Maybe they did, and I just couldn't see them!

Throughout the night, we had been hearing noises in many parts of the building, often in other rooms, so I suggested we all spread out to cover the entire club house. I naturally chose the hallway with the rattling closet door. However, as I walked down the dark hallway towards that

42

door, reality set in and I said into my recorder, "Oh hell, what am I doing back here…by myself!" Of course, if you want to get the best evidence, you have to go where there is the most activity—even if it creeps the hell out of you!

The hallway in a flash photo. The closet door is at
the end of the hall, the restrooms on the right.

Everyone got settled in their chosen spots and we all fell silent and waited. Several minutes later, I started hearing people talking. The voices sounded like they were coming from that closet, but I couldn't discount the possibility that sound could travel through air ducts or hallways. Hallie was in the next room, so I asked her to call out to see if anyone was talking. The question was passed along the length of the building to those at the far end, and back along the line to Hallie and then to me.

"No. No one has been talking," she reported.

That narrowed down the source, and I kept a watchful eye, and both ears, directed at that closet. The voices were faint, and weren't continuous, but I have no doubt the sounds were of people talking. Then the door started to rattle again, ever so slightly, but it was enough to get me to jump to my feet and run over to it. I stood right in front of the door, and Bob joined me, and we both heard footsteps. It was difficult to determine where the footsteps were coming from, or going to, but someone, or something, was walking around in the dark hallway with us. All of this activity continued for a few minutes, and then everything stopped as suddenly as it began.

We all reconvened in the central room and compared notes about what everyone heard and felt. All in all, it was much more than I had expected, but then again, I didn't realize the average death toll at golf courses. Taking into consideration what was on the land previously, as well, and you have all the ingredients and layers necessary for a potent haunting.

So in retrospect, rattling doors, footsteps, voices, cold spots, and EMF meters lighting up here is just par(anormal) for the course!

Note: A few months later, Gary told me that since the night of the investigation, most of the employees reported that everything "has been very quiet." However, one employee, "Ed," has had the opposite experience. For him, it seems that activity has greatly increased from that day.

As an example, Ed was at his desk and another employee, "Joe," was in the office with him. Suddenly, there was a loud pounding sound on Ed's desk, as if someone had just angrily slammed down his fist. Ed was stunned, as he didn't see any source for the sound. Joe—who was not facing the desk at that moment—asked if Ed was angry, as he was certain that Ed had just punched his desk.

Ed left his office right away, found Gary, and was obviously shaken as he said, "You will not believe what just happened!"

Why did the activity cease for some of the employees, but not for others? When we were in the ladies' offices the night of the investigation, I had asked whoever was there to please stop bothering them. Did they actually listen!? And is one or more of the spirits now centering their attention on Ed?

Ghosts truly have minds of their own, so who can ever know what they might be up to—especially after we trespass into their world...

Companions for Life
Kingston, NY

It was a warm, sunny afternoon in September of 2012 when Shin-ae was on her way to visit the graves of her grandparents at St. Mary's Cemetery in Kinston, NY. She was walking along a paved road in the cemetery when she saw something ahead.

In the road was an older man, probably in his 70s, and his motorcycle had fallen on top of him. Rushing to his aid, Shin-ae helped get his leg out from under the motorcycle and helped him to his feet.

The man had white hair, and was wearing a light, faded denim jacket and matching jeans, and a white shirt. He was about 5' 10" tall, and "had a slight belly." The fall might have injured him, as he walked with a limp. The man's motorcycle also appeared quite old, looking more like one of those earlier motorized bicycles than a modern motorcycle. Shin-ae had never seen anyone riding such an antique vehicle.

Reaching into his wallet, he pulled out a yellowed newspaper clipping of a woman's obituary.

"I'm looking for my companion," he said in a manner that evoked great pity for the man.

He said he had been looking for his "companion" for a very long time, but couldn't find her.

"Okay, I'll help you find the grave," Shin-ae told him.

Leaving the man standing by the motorcycle, which was still lying in the road, Shin-ae began searching the grave stones for the woman's name. Despite the cemetery being so large, it wasn't long before she found it, as it wasn't too far from her own grandparents' graves. Then she went back to the old man, put her arm around his waist to help him walk, and they slowly made their way to where his companion was buried.

He immediately knelt down and began to cry. Although Shin-ae wanted to know more about this man and the woman he obviously loved, she felt she should give him some privacy. Turning and walking away, she got no more than ten steps before she felt compelled to go back. However, when she turned, the old man was gone!

There was no way with his age and injury that he could have gotten out of sight so quickly. She looked in every direction, and then rushed back to where they had left the old motorcycle, but it was gone, too!

"I would have seen the man walk away," Shin-ae explained, still baffled and excited by what she witnessed. "And I certainly would have heard the motorcycle start up, and I would have seen it drive by me. The old man and his motorcycle simply disappeared in an instant!"

I asked Shin-ae some more detailed questions about this man, and she related the following:

He hadn't been wearing a helmet, and there wasn't one on the ground by the motorcycle. He was wearing dark shoes, possibly boots. His nose was slightly larger than average, and more rounded, and he had "large, intense eyes." His skin had a pinkish color, as if from exertion, and his hands were wrinkled, and "worn and calloused" from heavy use. He had no beard or mustache, and his white hair was "parted on the right and brushed over to the left." He was not wearing glasses or any jewelry.

I had two reasons for these questions—first of all, to get a better picture of the man, and also to find out just how much detail Shin-ae recalled. As she spoke, it was clear that this incident left such an impression on her, that the memory of that old man and his antique motorcycle was as vivid as if it had just happened. She said it was like a mental photographic image she still had of him.

I also asked if at any point she had felt fear, especially after he vanished, and was surprised by her response.

"No, I was never afraid. It did give me goose bumps, though, and I felt…content. I felt as though I had helped this man finally find his companion."

We discussed what an odd choice of words "companion" was to describe this woman. We also wondered how long he had searched for her, and, of course, whether they were now reunited.

If this is a ghost story, I would like to think it was one with a happy ending.

Hunt Country Furniture
Wingdale, NY

For almost twenty years, I have been indebted to the readers of my ghost books for bringing to my attention more haunted locations. Without all of your help, I probably wouldn't be currently writing Volume 12 of the *Ghost Investigator* series. The case of the Hunt Country Furniture store in Wingdale, NY is a prime example, as I learned of it from Irena Goss. Irena's sister is Aldona Pilmanis, who is a librarian at the Nyack library, where we all investigated for the story which appears in *Ghost Investigator Volume 11*.

In June of 2014, Irena and her family decided to get in the car and take a day trip in New York and Connecticut, and ended up at the Webatuck Craft Village in Wingdale, New York. As Irena had remembered the place from years ago, it was "once a thriving little village" of craft shops and restaurants, but sadly, most are now closed.

I should mention at this point, that if the name Wingdale sounds familiar, it may be because the little town was once the site of an infamous psychiatric hospital. Opened in 1924, by the 1950s there were over 5,000 patients and another 5,000 employees. Among its claims to infamy was that it was the first asylum in the United States to use insulin shock therapy; a brutal technique which repeatedly put patients into a coma, day after day, for months at a time. The asylum doctors later helped pave the way for the even more barbaric electroshock therapy and frontal-lobe lobotomies.

As more powerful antipsychotic drugs were developed and fewer patients were being institutionalized, the population at the hospital began to drop; finally leading to the place closing in 1994. Plans are currently underway to convert the buildings and property into an upscale housing community. Good luck with that!

Understandably, the loss of so many thousands of jobs in a small community was devastating, and the recent economic slowdown has not been kind to local independent craftsmen, either. However, one of the stores at the Webatuck Village has persevered since 1926: Hunt Country Furniture. Their showroom is located in a beautiful home built in 1747. Irena told me she "definitely felt an energy" to the place upon entering, and couldn't resist asking the assistant sales manager, Cathlee, "Have you experienced any paranormal activity while working here?"

Cathlee began to relate some amazing stories of things that had occurred over the decade she has worked there—too many for Irena to write down in her message to me. Instead, based upon Irena's strong recommendation, I contacted Cathlee and arranged to stop by one Saturday afternoon with my husband, Bob Strong.

When we arrived, we were immediately struck by all the picturesque 18th century buildings surrounded by woods, bordered by a sparkling river; not to mention the beauty and quality of the furniture. I have always loved working with wood (Zimmermann means carpenter, and there's a long line of carpenters on both sides of my family), so I could really appreciate the richness of the local hardwoods they use, and the craftsmanship that goes into every piece they make. I may sound like a commercial, but don't just take my word for it. How else could they have remained in business for 90 years?

We met Cathlee and Gail Richards, the sales manager, and we talked for a while about the history of the house, which was built by Ebenezer Preston (1727-1809) in 1747. I did some further research, and found that in 1749, he married Hannah Smith (1729-1816), and they had two children, also named Hannah and Ebenezer. In Preston's will, he lists the family farm and a sawmill as his main assets, but the family also generated income by using the house as an inn for farmers transporting their produce from Connecticut to the markets of New York.

The Hunt family began making their fine furniture here in 1926, eventually constructing a large factory on the hill behind the house. The craft village was their idea, and it grew to include many craftsmen, from silversmiths to potters to stained glass makers, as well as a charming restaurant, all housed in the old, historic buildings.

Cathlee began our tour by taking us up the main staircase. I had the impression of children on the staircase, but decided not to say anything and just listen to what Cathlee had to say. She then related a story about her 14-year-old daughter, who is very sensitive, and told Cathlee that she saw "a little girl in 18th century clothing" on the stairs. The girl looked quite real and even spoke; warning her daughter to "Watch out for that step." Had this girl tripped on that step and been injured in a fall—or worse?

The girl also said, "I don't like all of these people in my house. Why are they all here?" That day, there was a festival taking place, so the house was filled with many visitors. The spirit of the girl is obviously confused, and can't comprehend why strangers keep coming into *her* house. Cathlee's daughter has also seen a little boy, who she referred to as "the girl's brother." Hopefully, someone will be able to get through to these children and let them know that it's time to move on.

The house was much larger than I expected, and it is an amazing structure—the type of place I would love to live, minus the ghosts, of course. As I was looking at one of the seven fireplaces, Cathlee said her daughter believes something was hidden inside, but as it has been sealed off, we may never know. I would like to include a sledgehammer and sawzall in my gear bag for such occasions, but I fear I would not be invited on any more investigations!

We went down into the basement, and I commented that "It wasn't too high on the creepy scale." However, such was not the case with an outside staircase leading down to the basement. Members of the Hunt family had very recently related a story which took place when their grandparents lived there. A drunken man wandered onto the property one night and had fallen down those stairs. His body was found the next morning, as he had died from the fall. Such tragic and senseless accidents are often fodder for haunted activity. (And now that I think about it, I wonder if the little girl's warning about being careful on the stairs has some connection?)

The stairs where the drunken man fell to his death.

After our tour—during which I saw at least a dozen beautiful pieces of cherry wood furniture and cabinets I wanted!—we went back the office area, where the register is also located. Cathlee told us that when she first started to work here over ten years ago, she was at the register as someone was "explaining protocols and training me, and I look over this way and I see a form standing right here, peering around the corner. There were no features, just a dark form. My coworker continued to talk but I wasn't listening, wondering what *is* that!?"

Cathlee standing where the dark figure appeared.

Suddenly the figure moved like it was startled, as if it realized Cathlee could see it. Then it just disappeared. A few days later while walking by this area where the figure appeared, she wondered who it had been, and she "immediately got the name Phineas Culpepper." Shortly after, a member of the Hunt family came in, and Cathlee asked if the name Culpepper meant anything. The man looked surprised and puzzled at the question, but replied that it was the name of the high school from which he had graduated in Virginia.

"But you graduated from Pawling (NY) High School," Cathlee responded, certain that the family members had grown up and been educated locally.

The man responded that right before high school, the family had moved to Virginia for several years.

"Okay, so tell me why you asked that?" he said, obviously intrigued.

Cathlee explained the figure and the name coming to her, and without skipping a beat the man exclaimed, "That must have been my father letting you know he was here!"

We were then joined by Gail, and I asked if any customers had ever mentioned anything unusual. Gail recounted an incident when two women walked into the former carriage house next door, where discounted items are kept, and they came right back out because they felt very uncomfortable. I have to admit, my Ghost Investigator senses went on high alert when we went into that building, as well.

One day when Cathlee was working in the carriage house, she heard *and saw* a man on the staircase there. He was dressed in blue jeans, a black t-shirt, wore a gold chain, and "had an olive complexion and short, dark hair." She spoke up and said to him that she was sorry she hadn't noticed him sooner, and asked if he needed any help. And then he just vanished.

When she described the man to some of the craftsmen in the factory, they knew right away who she was talking about. He used to work at the factory, and actually lived in the carriage house. They insisted that Cathlee must have seen a picture of this man, because he had died!

In addition to the carriage house, other buildings nearby have had haunted activity, including the furniture factory, where a variety of sounds have also been heard, mostly in the form of phantom footsteps. These footsteps have been heard for many years, and have also been reported quite recently. Are the old craftsmen who worked here for so many years, having loved what they did, still walking the factory floor to keep an eye on things to make sure their standards of quality are still being met?

The carriage house, and the staircase where the deceased employee appeared.

The restaurant which used to be part of the craft village, the Buttonwood Café, was also in a beautiful house from the 1700s. There were many stories of spooky things happening there, but unfortunately, after the café closed the building was demolished. What a shame!

I asked Gail if she had ever experienced anything, and she replied that she "hears things, I don't see things." On many occasions she has come out of her office asking, "Can I help you?" as she clearly heard someone come in, but has found herself alone.

One day Gail was in her office with the door closed, and Cathlee was just a few feet away near the counter, when there were three loud knocks on the office door.

"I couldn't understand why Gail was in her office knocking on the door," Cathlee said. "When Gail came out of her office, I asked why she was knocking."

Not only had Gail *not* knocked on her office door, she also hadn't noticed the knocking!

While Cathlee waited on some customers, Gail took us for a quick tour of the factory. As Bob and I both love woodworking, we were intensely envious of everything from the quality of the hardwood lumber to the tools and machinery used to create such beautiful furniture. There's nothing like the smell of sawdust in the morning!

Gail pointed out the many areas where figures are seen and footsteps are heard. In one room we entered I got a chill and felt a strong presence, or perhaps several. This was the room where "the real, old world craftsmen" used to work. It definitely felt as though they had not all yet left the building.

We went to the office area where the staff frequently hears footsteps overhead, then went to the second floor above. I experienced that same "you're not alone" sensation, along with a rather tense feeling, and Gail concurred. I found myself taking quick, short breaths, for no obvious reason.

When we left that area and went into another room, I spun around as if I expected to see someone, or find something behind a door at the other end of the room. I asked what was behind the door, and Gail explained it was where all the old company records were kept. I'm sure there was a wealth of information to be discovered in there, especially about the staff members who still walk these rooms and hallways.

All in all, I believe many of the buildings in the Webatuck Village can lay claim spirits, and I wouldn't be surprised if more stories come to light. Why such places have so much paranormal activity is anybody's guess, but I have found time and again that they often have many layers stretching back numerous generations. Whether you are in the market for handmade furniture or other crafts, or are looking for something more otherworldly, you can't go wrong by visiting "Ghost Hunt" Country Furniture!

Do former residents remain in their home because
it looks like it did generations ago?

Illustrations of a Haunting
Averill Park, NY

Not too many ghost stories begin with an attack by a rabid fox, but for former comic book artist John, it was just the strange start to a day that ended even stranger.

It was a very hot summer day in 2013, and John's wife, who was six-months pregnant, and his 3-year-old daughter were in their pool. He was standing next to the pool, skimming out leaves. Out of the blue, a crazed fox charged at him, snapping its teeth, and latching onto his shorts. He was able to fend it off with a board, but the vicious animal fell into the pool with his wife and daughter. Miraculously, John got his family out of the pool, without anyone getting hurt or bitten. Once they were safely inside, John called 911. The police and animal control service arrived, and when the fox tried to attack them, it was shot several times and killed.

Needless to say, it was a very stressful day, so they decided to go out to dinner at one of their favorite restaurants in the town of Averill Park, New York. The place had been a blacksmith shop in the 1800s, and when the current owners were renovating it, they uncovered the original beams, tools, and some horseshoes, and decided to preserve all those elements in their restaurant.

They were seated on the first floor, and as 3-year-olds are prone to do, his daughter started running around. She kept trying to go upstairs, where there is another dining room. Even though John and his wife repeatedly told her she couldn't go up there, she insisted on going back to the staircase, because she wanted to see "Grandpa."

"It didn't register at first," John told me. "She stood there looking up that staircase and kept saying, 'Hi, Grandpa,' over and over."

Was there a customer dining upstairs who looked like her grandfather?

"My daughter never met my father," John explained. "In fact, I never even knew him, either, because he died when I was only two months old."

However, what was really shocking was that way back in the 1950s, John's father and mother lived at the top of those same stairs in an apartment, when the place was a private residence! His daughter had no idea her grandpa used to live there, yet here she was, happily talking to a man who had died decades before she was born.

Had the extreme danger that John and his family faced that day from the rabid fox prompted his father to let them know that he was watching over them? Had his father even gone so far as to protect them from a possibly fatal bite? At the very least, on such a traumatic day, it was comforting to think that loved ones who have passed on may still be with us.

While John can't say for sure what happened that night in the restaurant, he is open to the idea of spirits, as he had another encounter. About ten years ago, he was working the night shift at his job, and when he got home he was often "keyed up" and couldn't get to sleep. To unwind, he would often take long bike rides around the Troy, NY area.

One night, he decided to go to the Evergreen Cemetery in Wynantskill, NY, to watch the sunrise. He rode up to the top of a hill, where the dawn would break over a mausoleum. Despite the somewhat creepy surroundings, the cemetery was quiet and peaceful, and watching a beautiful sunrise was just the type of relaxation he needed. Unfortunately, the last thing he was able to do was relax.

"There was an awful chill," he explained. "Someone was watching me, and I kept turning around to see who was there."

At one point when he looked behind him, he saw a faint light. As the surrounding area was very dark, he couldn't exactly tell where the light was coming from.

"Then I saw it was actually two orange lights, like eyes. I thought maybe it was an owl, but there wasn't a tree where these orange eyes were, and they were about eight to ten feet above the ground!"

As John moved from left to right, so did the eyes. Wherever he went in the cemetery, they followed.

"It freaked me out!" he declared, certain that whatever it was, it was *not* natural.

There are also local accounts of people seeing a lady in a black dress on that cemetery hill, so perhaps the chill and glowing eyes are somehow connected with this mysterious phantom.

While everything is open to interpretation, for former comic book artist John, these two stories are excellent illustrations of a haunting.

Return to McGarrah's Inn
Monroe, NY

I first wrote about McGarrah's Stagecoach Inn in in 2006, for *Ghost Investigator Volume 6*. For those of you who don't own that book—although I can't imagine why not!:)—the structure was first built in the 1790s, possibly over the site of an even older building. In addition to being an inn, it housed the oldest Masonic Lodge in the state (third oldest in the country), and today is owned and operated by the Cornerstone Masonic Historical Society.

Its history of paranormal activity goes back many years, and includes everything from footsteps to full-bodied apparitions. I have had many experiences there over the years, with the most dramatic being a very tall, dark figure in the basement that looked so real I thought it was an actual person, until it suddenly vanished.

Suffice it to say, when journalist MJ Goff asked if I would like to conduct another investigation with my ghost hunting partners, Mike

Worden and Barbara Roth Bleitzhofer, for an article she was writing, I didn't need to be asked twice. We arranged to meet one night in November of 2013, and we were also joined by Barb's friend Duane Smith, who has been on several paranormal adventures with us. MJ had arrived earlier to interview Dave Roman, a member of the lodge, and when we arrived he also filled us in on some of the latest activity.

Barb had already experienced her own unique form of activity days before, in the form of two female spirits who came to her. One was "older, in darker clothes with an apron, and very husky," and "the thinner one was in her mid-thirties, wearing brighter clothes, with an apron." Their names were Carol and Elsie. It is not uncommon for Barb to already start receiving messages and images once an investigation is scheduled. It's good to know that the spirits are as anxious to get started as we are!

When Barb first arrived—but hadn't yet entered—she also felt that two slaves had died in the basement. One of the theories about McGarrah's was that it had been a stop on the Underground Railroad. But more on that later.

Mike took this photo of Duane and Barb at the start of the investigation.

There's a large, old safe in the room by the side-door entrance, and when Barb touched it, her "fingers burned, like an electric shock," and she heard the name Carl being shouted. The lights on my K2 EMF meter began flashing, and I asked if anyone's cell phone was on, as they can make the meter go off. However, everyone checked, and their phones were off. We were later to find out from Dave that there is significance to the name Carl, as he is the master of the lodge! Barb believed that whatever spirit was attached to that safe did not like the fact that a woman was touching it, and was trying to alert the master of lodge to stop her.

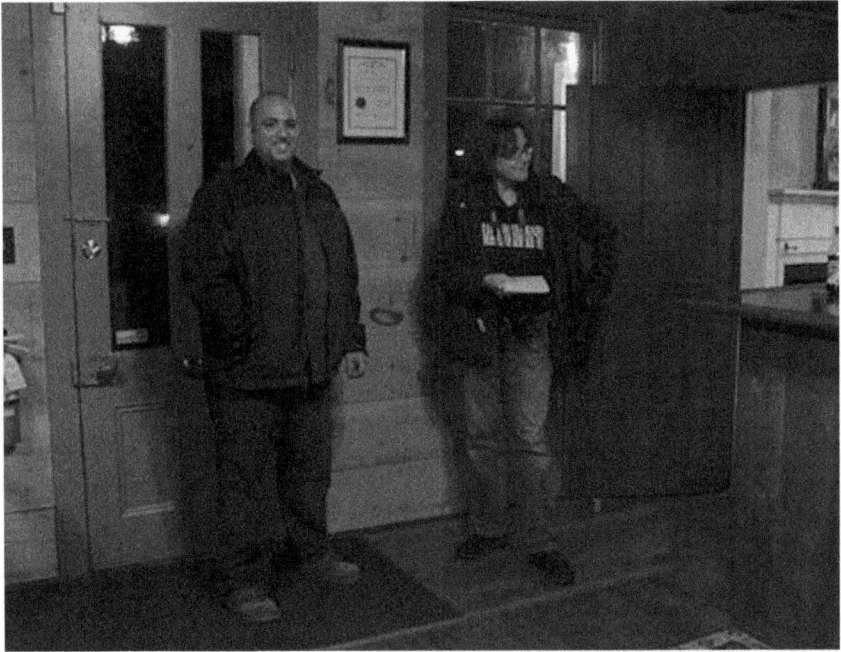

Dave and MJ

We went into the large room on the first floor, to the left of the front door, and as my meter lit up again, Barb had some very unpleasant feelings.

"Did they use this as some sort of a medical hospital?" she asked me. "People were sick in here. Really sick."

I didn't know of the building being used for such purposes, but we were to discover that she was right. I asked Dave if the place was ever used as some type of a hospital, and was quite surprised to find out that it had, and even more surprised to find out in what capacity. Apparently, the place had been used "as a sanitarium for the mentally insane" in the early 1900s!

"How did I never know this?" I asked rhetorically, wondering why no one on my previous investigations had mentioned this very important fact.

No, this isn't a game of Simon Says. Both Barb and Mike began experiencing head pains on the first floor, as Duane looks on.

Dave then showed us a photograph he had taken at McGarrah's of a little girl with a doll. The only problem was that when he took the picture, the girl didn't have a doll with her. In fact, no one had a doll that night. Barb felt that the doll had belonged to a child who died here and was still trying to play with living children. Another psychic who investigated the house had claimed that she saw a little girl running around, and up and down a staircase. When she said this, this woman was pointing to an empty corner of a room where there was no staircase. However, there *used* to be stairs there, and I can personally attest to that as they were still there when I first visited McGarrah's in 2006. Many people had reported hearing footsteps going up and down that staircase.

Shortly after speaking about this, Barb told me, "They want you to come up."

I asked for some clarification, and she replied that "they" wanted *me* specifically, to come upstairs. While I am more than happy to oblige such paranormal invitations, I responded that I would go upstairs soon, after I finished the first floor. And I'm glad I waited, because in the next room Barb felt that there was a man from the 1890s time period who had lost a leg. He still walks through the house with the telltale sound of his prosthetic limb. This one-legged man would make his presence known in a dramatic way later on that evening.

When we finally went upstairs, there was a strange feeling. Mike immediately said he felt "off balance" and we all agreed something just wasn't right. In the bedroom on the front right (as you are looking at the front of the house), both Duane and Barb had the sense of a man "with a bad stomach" dying in that room—and he didn't like the fact that we were there.

I asked Barb how many people she thought had died in the house over the years, and her quick response was, "Eighty-six. I was going to say about a hundred, but I heard eighty-six." With numbers like that, there's certainly plenty of fodder for all kinds of hauntings!

We then went to the room in the back of the house on the right, and Mike saw the door to that room move on its own. Both he and MJ heard the door scraping along the floor as it moved. At this point, I realized we were in the room where I had filmed a story with the local News 12 television crew. We had all heard a bizarre and chilling moaning sound that night, and when the reporter, Diana Russini, and I went into the adjoining bathroom, the toilet flushed on its own, causing us to practically jump out of our skins!

As everyone discussed what was going on, I looked out the door to the staircase and could swear I saw someone moving on the stairs, but we were all accounted for in the room (Dave had left before we came upstairs). I asked that if someone was there they needed to give us a clear sign. Duane immediately heard someone crying, possibly a child. MJ and Barb also heard the eerie sound. Activity really begin to pick up, as Mike started feeling very ill, and Duane could hear people having a

64

conversation, although he couldn't make out what they were saying. It was all very tense and somewhat chaotic for several minutes.

Right after I thought I saw someone in the hall, Mike took this infrared photo. It wasn't until he got home and viewed the image on his computer that he realized there was a thick mist in the hall at that moment!

As many of the readers of my books know, I often get some crazy images or words in my head during investigations. Some turn out to be amazing validations, and others, well, they just seem crazy. But as ridiculous as they usually sound, I just come out and say them for the digital recorder, and for anyone I am with on the investigation, just in case we later find some connection to the case.

With this in mind, when we went into the Masonic meeting room on the second floor, I kept hearing something in my head over and over. It wasn't anything threatening or spooky; quite the opposite. It was, in fact, a line from the Cowardly Lion's song in the *Wizard of Oz*, "If I were king of the forest." That line played over and over in my head, so I just told everyone what I was hearing. Barb thought that perhaps the "man in charge thinks he's the king." I confessed I had no idea what it meant, but it got stranger.

As the king imagery continued, I thought of the line from Shakespeare, "Uneasy lies the head that wears a crown." Before I could say it out loud, Mike said that he was feeling "uneasy." Coincidence? Maybe, but then again, maybe not.

Thinking out loud, I suggested that perhaps someone there was named King. Duane then interjected a humorous note and said that perhaps I had found Elvis! In fact, the entire mood of the room shifted from tense and uneasy, to something I characterized as "more playful." Whoever the king was, he had a sense of humor.

Mike and MJ in the meeting room.

The mood changed once again when we went into the attic. The tension definitely returned and we all got the sense that unpleasant things had happened there. The uneasy sense continued into Dave's office, and we all wondered how he could work in there!

Barb and Mike encountering something disturbing in the attic.

In the old Masonic meeting room on the third floor, I once again would swear that I saw someone on the staircase. At the same time, Duane and Barb heard something.

"Did you hear that?" Mike asked, not a minute later. "There was something out there." (On the staircase.)

"That's what I'm saying!" I replied, certain that I had seen something, but not at all certain what it was that I saw.

I hurried out to the staircase and asked if anyone else was there. I thought I heard a voice, but no one else did. I talked to Mike about what he saw, and he confirmed a dark figure had moved along the staircase.

"And he was moving very fast," Mike added.

"It's a kid," Barb said.

"That was my impression, that it was a child," Mike agreed.

There was silence for a few moments, and then at about the 2 minute mark of track 17 of the audio files, there was a clear female voice that we all heard, and was also recorded. It sounded like a girl saying something like "mamma," but we couldn't be sure. We also couldn't be absolutely certain that the voice hadn't come from someone out on the street, but we were fairly sure it had originated inside the building. We waited for the voice again, but there was just silence.

The next stop on our investigation was the basement, where I had seen the tall, dark figure eight years earlier. One of the creepier parts of the basement is the "Red Room," so named because the walls are painted red.

"Not a good room, Linda. I think they held them in here," Barb said as she entered.

"Held who?" I asked.

"People are pacing, going foot to foot," she continued, moving as if she was in shackles, which meant they were either prisoners, slaves, or people who needed to be restrained for some reason—such as the mentally disturbed patients? "And I hear deep voices…very deep."

She then started mumbling something incoherent, and I was only able to pick out an occasional word, such as "blurry." I knew her mind was elsewhere, listening to who-knows-what, but I needed to gently get her back to focus.

"You're not making any sense, Barb."

"It's going blurry. It's going to go all blurry, and then you're just going to keel over, they're saying. And you have to go down low. Get down low. Oh, Linda, this is really not a good room," she said, in obvious discomfort. "It's very strange in here. They said their eyes go blurry and then they just go down. They go down."

"Were they drugged?" I asked.

"Almost like gassed or drugged or something," she replied. "And they're tired, they are very tired."

Mike took this infrared photo of Barb sinking to the floor
of the Red Room as she describes the drugged feeling.

MJ suggested that if this place was a stop on the Underground Railroad, perhaps the sick and starving runaway slaves were completely exhausted when they arrived, with many collapsing, and some not surviving. There are remnants of tunnels leading out of the basement, which does lend credibility to the idea that this place may indeed have been used to help slaves escape to freedom.

Barb thought it could be part of the explanation, as whoever these people were, they needed to speak very softly and stay down low, as if they were hiding. Could the blurred vision and "keeling over" been symptoms of some disease with which a group was afflicted? Or, is her feeling of being drugged accurate, and had something to do with unruly patients from the days of it being the mental hospital; patients who may have been placed down here and sedated?

I noticed during this entire time, Mike was standing back by the door.

"I don't want to be in this room," he stated. "Being in there, I…just don't like it."

That was our general consensus for the Red Room, and while we were temporarily relieved to exit it, there were more bad vibes awaiting us in the back room. That was where I had been standing when I saw the dark figure in the doorway. As Barb passed through that doorway, she kind of groaned and just kept saying, "No, no, no." None of us liked this room, but we went back upstairs to get more equipment to explore it further.

I began by asking if anyone was buried down there, which is one of the rumors. Mike added that we needed a clear sign, and as we sat in the creepy darkness, he heard knocking from somewhere above us. He invited whoever it was to "come closer" and make another sound, but we waited and waited, and nothing further happened. I was then surprised that Barb suggested we move back to the Red Room, which we did.

On my audio recording, I'm stating that we are back in the Red Room, and as I was listing the equipment we had set up, the Trifield meter starting squealing as I was saying the word "Trifield," which certainly caught our attention! We waited for several long minutes, asking a series of questions with no response, and then things started happening.

As Barb reported that she was hearing voices, Mike said that something was moving behind him. The EMF meters kept registering high readings, as well. And there was something odd going on with the temperature. Barb and Duane felt very hot, while the rest of us found the room to be quite chilly. This little flurry of activity lasted for several minutes, but the most interesting thing that occurred was when Barb said that "a very tall man walks around down here." As the dark figure I had seen was well over six feet, I suspected she was seeing the same entity!

Even though we had planned on making the basement our last stop, we all couldn't resist going back to the bedroom on the second floor where we heard the voice. Barb immediately saw the torso and head of a figure run through the hallway by the stairs, just as Mike and I had seen earlier. And we could chalk up another bizarre occurrence, as Barb and Mike both experienced their feet hurting! I always say the symptoms of the haunting are connected to the life of the spirit and the message it is trying to convey, so perhaps this was one such message, although we didn't know how it tied in, other than as Barb suggested, "there was a lot of movement and walking."

Unfortunately, there were a lot of noises from the outside—such as a big flock of geese and way too many trucks—so it was difficult to conduct a quiet stakeout. But at one point, it sounded like the front door opened, which would not have been possible, as it was locked. I decided to go back to the meeting room where I kept getting "king" references, so I could hear things from a different angle, and also because that room really intrigued me that night.

Sitting in the meeting room by myself, I felt an intense male presence. It wasn't threatening by any means, but it was quite strong. Over and over I just kept hearing the word "king," but always in a lighthearted way. And for some reason, I later characterized the man as British, although in retrospect I don't know what prompted me to say that. While there was no outward evidence on either audio or video, I was certainly convinced that someone was in that room with me.

When I returned to the bedroom, I found out I had missed some impressive evidence. Barb had her laser grid set up (which consists of a laser pointer that disperses a wide pattern of points of light to detect any motion or something blocking the lights) and as they were all watching, the lights flickered and faded almost to darkness. They expected the batteries were going dead—even though Barb had just installed fresh batteries—but then the lights grew bright again and remained steady. This all occurred without anyone touching the laser pointer, and we had never seen this occur before.

As we sat quietly, I recalled an investigation Mike and I had conducted in 2007 (see *Ghost Investigator: Volume 7*) in a house where a suicide had occurred. We had had some extreme reactions from our Trifield meter in one room, when we weren't even inside that room. I wondered what was making me think of that case, and the fact that it had involved a suicide seemed to be the primary reason.

"Anyone have any sense of a suicide?" I asked our group.

Barb reminded me that earlier in the evening, she had stood at the railing to the staircase and said she felt as if she was dropping. Then Mike

71

said when he was taking a photograph while leaning over that railing, he suddenly felt nervous. Had someone fallen down the stairs or over that railing, either intentionally, accidentally, or by being pushed? We have no record of such a death, but in the building's long and varied history, anything is possible. And one other curious thing: as we were discussing this, MJ said the grid pattern of lights suddenly was blocked in the hallway, "as if someone went by."

We spent quite a while longer in that bedroom without anything else happening, but just as I said, "Nothing is happening," the laser light dimmed again!

I decided to sit on the staircase for a while, as that was where a lot of the action was taking place. I didn't feel completely at ease, but there wasn't anything dramatic—until a cold breeze felt "like it went right through me" and "made my heart all fluttery." Perhaps it was a draft, but I can tell you, that was one hell of a bone-chilling, all-engulfing draft, and I chose to get up and move away from the staircase.

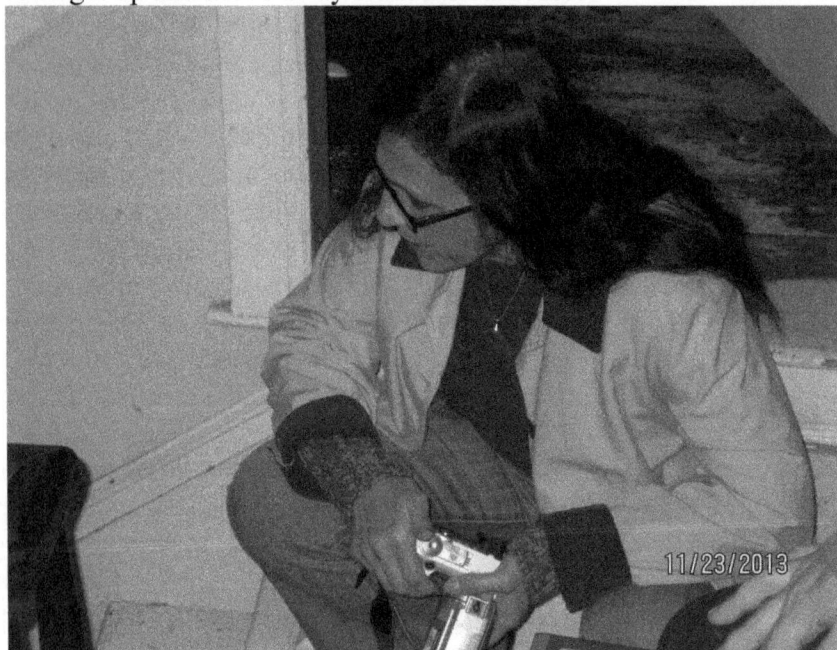

Barb took this photo of me on the staircase.

I invited/challenged Mike to try that spot, and he is never one to back away from a paranormal challenge.

"How's it feeling down there?" I asked.

"It feels…a little different," he replied after a slight hesitation, just as the grid light went completely dark and then brightened again. "And my leg is trembling. It's actually vibrating!"

I went to take a look, and sure enough, his right leg was visibly trembling, and it had started the instant the light went out.

"That's weird!" I exclaimed, really surprised that it was vibrating so much that it was clearly visible.

"Could it be the one-legged man?" Barb asked, referring to the spirit she had encountered earlier in the night.

"Whoa, did you just hear that!" I said excitedly, as Mike and I heard a loud noise below us. "Someone is downstairs."

As I was explaining the knocking and sounds of movement, it happened again.

"I heard that!" Duane said.

I called downstairs, but no one replied. We mentioned the one-legged man again, and the spasms in Mike's leg got worse. It took several long minutes for the uncomfortable vibrations in his leg to stop. Once it was over, I kidded Barb about a comment she had made just before this whole incident began.

"You had to tell whoever is here to go and touch Mike, didn't you?"

"Well, they listened to her," Mike said laughing.

"Sorry, Mike," Barb said.

"Hey, I'll take one for the team any time," he replied. He's a true ghost hunter!

Following this, there was a long, quiet lull, and I commented on how the "activity comes and goes."

"It's like they want us to know they are in control," Mike said.

A second after he spoke, there was another knocking or banging sound from the first floor which we all heard, and this one was loud enough to be picked up on my digital recorder.

A few minutes later, I was about to ask if any of the former patients were present, but before I could speak the light dimmed again, and this time we all felt the air suddenly turn freezing cold.

"And that just came *up* the stairs," Mike pointed out, which is contrary to the fact that cold air is supposed to sink, not go up unless there was a fan or breeze propelling it, which of course, there was not. At the same moment, a dog right outside began the most eerie and intense howling.

"Is that dog being punished?" Barb asked with concern.

We listened very carefully, because we all are big-time animal lovers, and if someone was hurting a dog, we would have descended on the perpetrator in a heartbeat. But the dog seemed to just be freaking out, howling and whining as if it was very frightened. We looked outside but couldn't see anything, and the awful sound stopped as suddenly as it had started. It was all very upsetting.

We went back downstairs and sat at the tables discussing what had occurred that night. When I mentioned the one-legged man, there was a metallic tapping sound.

"Where did that sound come from?" I asked.

"It was right behind you," Mike responded.

"Great!" I exclaimed sarcastically, wondering if the spirit of the one-legged man was next to me and would start making my leg muscles twitch, but fortunately I was spared that discomfort.

Nothing else occurred after that, which was fine by us as the long hours of tension had taken their toll. If you have never been on a ghost hunt where paranormal activity was taking place, it's hard to describe the mental, emotional, and physical impact it can have.

Not that I'm complaining! If I got a call with an invitation to a ghost hunt right now, I would once again return to Mcgarrah's.

Heaven on Earth?

What goes around, comes around, in more ways than one. The saying applies to both the spiritual world, as well as the mundane, as this case illustrates.

The paranormal happenings at Heaven on Earth Natural Foods in Pine Bush, New York, were brought to my attention by "Phyllis," who attended the UFO Fair in town in April of 2014. And the reason I was in Pine Bush that day speaking about my UFO books, was because during all the years I have been lecturing on ghosts, people in the audiences would also tell me their UFO stories, which inspired my research into local UFO sightings. In short, the ghost stories brought me to UFOs, which has come back around to bringing me to more ghost stories!

In terms of the spiritual implications of the saying, it is clear from years of ghost investigations that what people do in their lifetimes—both to themselves and to others—comes back around to impact them, and others, after death. You may think your actions don't matter, but everything has a price—and one way or another someone has to pay it, even generations later.

When Phyllis emailed me some information about the store, she explained that she had worked there for several years and had encountered some energies that were "pretty extreme in the basement," as well as some milder disturbances upstairs. Things would fall off of shelves (always the top shelf), and an intense presence often made it difficult for her to remain in the store. She felt that there were potentially dark secrets involving the old building, and truths wanting to be revealed; possibly involving a former owner in the distant past, children, and a slave. She had tried researching the history of the structure, but the records did not go back very far, and written records rarely reveal what went on behind closed doors—or in locked basements.

An early 1900s postcard of Main Street, with the line pointing to the current location of the store, and a Google Earth image of the present-day view.

The store had very recently been sold to Val and Keith, and she felt that the atmosphere felt different since they took over—and many customers had also commented on the shift—but all was not quiet. According to Phyllis, shortly after they opened, Keith, who is a corrections officer, "was going downstairs" and "there was a key that had appeared laying on the floor between the bottom of the stairs and the cooler...an old rusted shackle key (out of the blue)."

How did the antique key suddenly end up there, and why had it appeared for Keith? Was it a message for the man who keeps people locked up for a living? Or as Phyllis suggested, was it time to unlock the truth?

Other strange things happened to Keith within the first few weeks, including witnessing the basement door opening by itself. Recently, an entire shelf, which had been securely attached to the wall, fell down when no one was near it. On the other side of the store near the refrigerators— where many people have sensed a presence—a bag of bulgur suddenly came off the shelf and hit him! Val has not experienced anything of this nature so far—nor does she want to!—but she does believe something strange is going on.

I was certainly intrigued by all the information, especially as I had been to the store several times over the years. As a vegetarian, I love eating at the Pure City restaurant with its totally meatless menu, which is just a few doors down, and would often stop in the health food store afterwards. I can't say that I ever had any dramatic encounters on any of these visits, but in retrospect, I can say it wasn't the most hospitable atmosphere in there—although the staff was always friendly.

A couple of weeks after Phyllis' email, I was in Pine Bush one Saturday and dropped in the store to introduce myself. People can understandably be hesitant to arrange a ghost investigation, not knowing what it entails, especially with all the crazy shows on television that often don't represent paranormal researchers in the best light. I spoke with Val and explained what I do, and we decided to arrange an investigation for the following Friday evening after they closed.

I called Barbara Roth Bleitzhofer to see if she wanted to join Bob and I. When I told her where we were going, she related that years ago she and her husband went in the store, but she had to leave because of the powerful, unpleasant feelings. I didn't tell her what anyone had been experiencing, but I already knew we were in for an interesting night.

Of course, Bob, Barb, and I had to have dinner at Pure City while we waited for the store to close, and then we grabbed our gear and met with Val, Keith, Phyllis, and Val's mother and sister. We decided to jump right in and have Keith show us around and explain what had been happening. Barb immediately began to feel "pressure and pain" in her head, along with the feeling of being pushed away, as if someone didn't want us there—which certainly wouldn't be the first time spirits wanted us gone!

We went back behind the freezers into the kitchen area, where the feeling grew even stronger. There was a palpable energy there, for sure, and when I asked Barb if it was due to an event or an individual, she simply replied, "It's him."

"Did it used to go up here?" she asked Keith, motioning with her hands as if there were steps in front of her. "Was there a staircase, and is there a second floor?"

"There is a second floor," Keith replied. There had been a staircase to the second floor at one time, but he wasn't exactly sure where it had been located.

At this point, I should mention that Barb had called me earlier in the day to tell me she had already sensed a male presence of "a former boarder" who lived there in relatively recent times. She could even describe his brown hair, his tall, lean frame, his clothing, and age range of 39-50, "although he looked younger than he was." She also told me he made a lot of tapping sounds, and would often sigh loudly. Keith confirmed that he often heard someone tapping in that area, and had also heard the sighing. Phyllis added that she, too, had heard the deep sighing, which was one of the more unnerving things she had experienced during the time she worked there.

"He doesn't realize that this isn't his anymore," Barb explained about the discontented spirit. "It's like, 'What are all these people doing? Why are they in *my* spot?' He just has a pissed off attitude."

"Did he pass away here?" I asked.

"I think he might have."

Barb went on to describe his nervous energy, which leads him to make all the tapping sounds, as well as knock objects off of shelves—

which, of course, is one of the inexplicable things that happens most often here.

"He's not violent," Barb added. "He just doesn't see this as your store. And I think he died in a way that made him not realize that he is dead."

"Natural causes?" I asked.

"Feels like a heart attack," she replied.

"Do you know if they used to rent rooms upstairs?" I asked Keith.

"They rent rooms upstairs right now," he said, and have been renting rooms for many years. So the idea of a boarder passing away there is certainly plausible.

We also talked about the shift in the atmosphere, and Keith acknowledged that customers have told them they "breathe easier" in the store now. Barb believes this male spirit is more at ease with Keith and Val, "although he still isn't happy. But I blame that on his death. He does know he is dead, but he is not accepting of it." That lack of acceptance is also something we have encountered time and time again, with the new homeowners or occupants often suffering the consequences of the unhappy spirit.

Keith then handed Barb the old key he had found, and she said she felt herself "going back and back through layers" of time. I asked what it had been used for, and she responded right away, "Locking up the provisions," but she felt there may have been hidden meaning to that description she heard. There was a lot of negativity around the key, due to the angry man who had owned it. And there was another odd sensation connected with that key.

"There had to be a baby somehow involved, as I feel like I should be rocking it back and forth," Barb described, as she swayed from side to side. "There have been babies lost here."

Clutching the key between her hands, Barb's expression changed several times as she tried to process all the sensations flowing from it.

"I'm beginning to wonder if this was used for cuffs, as both of my wrists are hurting" she finally said, completely unaware that Phyllis had previously characterized it as a "shackle key." Barb then further explained the many uncomfortable and frightening feelings of being locked up which were associated with this key.

"Do you carry this key around?" Barb asked Keith.

"No, I never do," he replied.

"Good!" she quickly replied, clearly relieved that he wasn't in contact with the potent energy of the antique key.

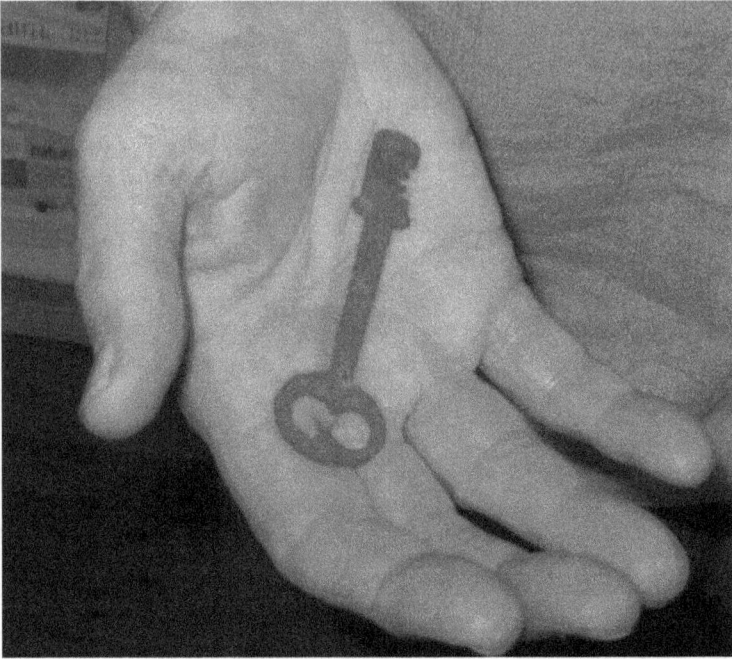

We discussed just who could have been locked up and why, and Barb believed that the man who owned this key was someone who "took the law into his own hands. And it makes me nervous, because whoever did this had the power to get away with it. When people saw this man it made them nervous, because they knew what he could do."

"So why is the key here?" I asked.

"Because of whatever is in the basement," she replied with a distressed look, as she had been avoiding going down there.

My next entry on the digital recorder was to report that, "We are heading down to the basement…those of us who want to go." Right away, I knew that this was one of the more sinister basements I have encountered, and considering what I do, that's saying a lot! You can hear on the recording that Barb is taking several deep breaths as we descended the stairs, bracing herself for whatever—or whoever—awaited us.

"Uh, oh, I want to start crying," Barb blurted out, obviously upset.

She saw someone "huddled in the corner" in the back of the basement, and my EMF meter was going off in that area. She felt it was a place of punishment and great fear. I asked if she sensed children or adults that were held here, and Barb quickly replied it was a woman she saw, and this woman—named Betty, or Betty Ann—was even more frantic because her baby had been taken away from her, and she kept asking, "Where is David?" Were pieces of the puzzle starting to come together, or were there just more puzzles to be solved?

Barb and I in the corner of the basement.

There was another room in the basement that appeared to have an old coal chute, and a well that had been filled in and capped. Barb believed that groups of people used to meet in this room—for nefarious purposes—possibly even the KKK, which was once very active throughout the Hudson Valley. Barb considered this, as she saw the woman in the corner having dark skin, while the "key holder most definitely did not" and appeared to wield power like a judge. At the very least, "they were angry men who were not part of the judiciary system."

Keith and Barb examining the well cap.

I then used a new piece of equipment; a fiber optic digital camera with a long cable. I stuck it in a hole in the well cap and just saw some dirt, rocks, and some modern debris. Barb believed there were things to discover down that well, but they were better left buried. I also snaked the cable back into some cracks in the walls and found bits of cloth and indications of a second, possibly older foundation.

Then I slipped the cable in the wall above where Barb saw the frightened, imprisoned woman, and at first just saw rock, mortar, and tangles of small plant roots, but then the light reflected off of something dark and shiny. At first I considered it might be some type of beetle, but upon closer inspection it was perfectly smooth and polished, like an oval stone or glass that may have been used for jewelry. Had someone hidden something precious to them in this wall?

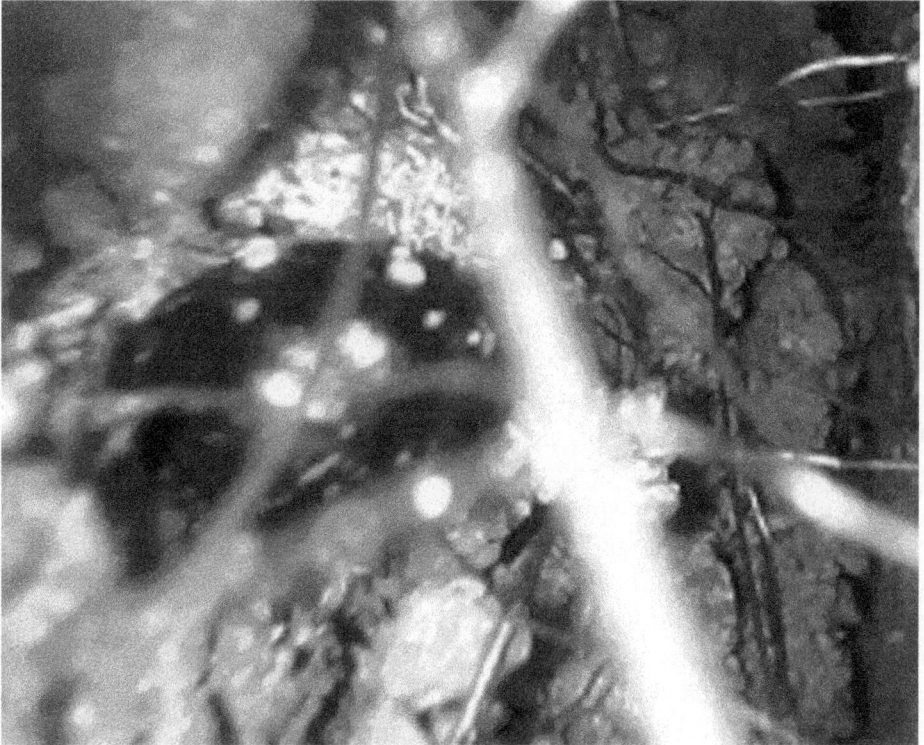

The dark, oval object. Is it animal, vegetable, or mineral?

Of course, my curiosity made me want to grab a sledgehammer or crowbar and start bashing away at the old foundation, but I had to content myself with just taking pictures of the unusual object. It very much reminded me of a piece of rainbow obsidian that I have, with the same deep black, and flashes of color, depending upon how the light hits it. Perhaps it was just a piece of anthracite coal that someone had cut and polished, but unless I can figure out a non-destructive way to get it out of the wall, we will never know. In any event, it was unusual, and Barb did feel that it somehow could have been connected to the woman.

When we went back upstairs, we heard some of the tapping sounds in the area of the refrigerator, where many people have felt a presence. There is bank of plastic dispensers there filled with grains and beans, and it sounded like someone was tapping on those dispensers. I felt very uncomfortable in that area, and Phyllis said that one day a customer had to sit down on the floor there, as she was suddenly overcome by a very strong feeling. Could this be the actual spot where the man had passed away?

Phyllis also told us about someone she knew who had lived upstairs. He had experienced a lot of unexplained activity there, and he had characterized it as being "dark," in terms of the negativity surrounding it. That may all be connected with the same unhappy man who lived and died here, and is making others pay for his refusal to move on.

We all spent some time discussing ways of trying to clear the spirits from the building, or at least make them more content and quiet. Various cleansing techniques don't always work—and, in fact, can initially make things worse—but I am a big advocate for the theory that the living have a great advantage over the dead. I believe that calm, yet forceful, persistence can eventually make the spirits literally "see the light" and leave.

Perhaps our investigation that night did have a positive impact on the place. Barbara and I dropped in a few months later and spoke to Keith, who said that "things had been quiet" since we were there. Barb agreed that it felt very different, in a good way. If these ghosts have been trying to get their messages to the living via all the paranormal activity, then perhaps they have been contented by the knowledge that their messages were received. Hopefully, all will be peaceful from now on, and that serene atmosphere will truly make it feel like heaven on earth.

Fleeing Pine Bush

I was contacted by "Bill," who used to live in an apartment in a house in Pine Bush, but was forced to leave his home because of all the frightening paranormal activity. I asked him to describe what had happened to him and his family, and he sent me the following description, which I have edited to maintain his anonymity.

"I'll try to explain my story best I can. Me and my wife and daughter, who was two at the time, are originally from [town deleted], New York. We were married this past October and moved to an apartment in Pine Bush on [street deleted] in November. I work in [town and occupation deleted] and worked overnights midnight to 8am so my wife and daughter were alone at night. My wife started saying she heard footsteps at night, like someone's walking around the bedroom. I dismissed it thinking it's just the floor settling or something. Over the next couple months it was the same stuff, plus my daughter's toys in the attic went off randomly a lot.

"But since we moved, we always were creeped out by our daughter's bedroom in the corner, it just didn't feel right in there, and in the laundry room next to it, but again, we just dismissed it. Our daughter never slept in there anyway, she always ended up in our bed. It always felt like someone was watching you when you did the dishes. Both me and my wife would look at the reflection in the window in front of the sink to see if anyone was there. We were never at ease.

"My wife gave birth to our son in March in [town deleted], so we stayed for a couple weeks with our parents. I randomly would go to the apartment and clean up for my son's arrival and set up the baby stuff. One night I was doing dishes, and from the corner of my eye, I saw what looked like the toilet paper roll falling down and bouncing off the sink and toilet, then the floor, but there wasn't anything there (the bathroom was attached to kitchen). I know I saw a bright, white thing bounce down from the sink, but couldn't explain it. As soon as I looked over and got scared, my daughter's toys in the attic went off over and over, so I got the heck out of there.

"I called my wife and explained the situation, and she admitted to seeing what I learned is called a white orb in the bedroom. She just didn't want to tell me, because she knows how scared of the paranormal I am. I just let it go, and we moved back with our son. Our daughter wanted to start sleeping in her bedroom to be a big girl, so we agreed and set up a baby monitor.

"Well, things got crazy from that day on. Our daughter started talking about 'Green Mommy' and scary shadows. Green Mommy was her friend who talked to her, and we found out she called her Green Mommy because she wore green clothes. The shadows would scare her.

"I was on vacation from work and home for two weeks, and we would both wake up and hear a woman's voice over the monitor, but could never understand what she said, and we would run into the room. Usually, I'd wake up and hear the voice, then my daughter would start to cry and I'd go in, but there was nothing there. One morning, we were still in bed and our daughter was in her room playing, and we were listening over the monitor. We started hearing her talking to someone, and we heard two voices—the woman and our daughter. That was so scary.

"My family was over for first time to see the apartment and we went to the UFO fair. I began to explain the creepy things, but they think it's stupid and everyone just mocked it, and would pretend to be ghosts, etc.

"Starting that night, things got too much for us. I woke up in the middle of the night, and I proceeded to watch the bedroom door open by itself. I looked up, hoping it was my daughter, but no one was there. Then a minute later, my daughter walked in. It was almost like the ghost opened the door for her. The next night, my wife watched the door close. And she saw a white orb zoom around my son.

"He slept in his car seat next to the bed. My wife looked to check on him, and she saw it in front of him, then it zoomed away. The next day I had enough. I was terrified. Then my wife was getting a bath ready for my daughter and left the bathroom, my daughter was in the living room, and walked to the bathroom. The second my daughter walked into the bathroom the whole shower caddy (which was secure) crashed down.

"Then I was in there while she was getting her bath, and she looks up towards me and screams in horror, and says, "Scary shadows!" and points to the ceiling behind me in the corner. That was our breaking point, so we packed up and went back to [town deleted] that night. I started looked at pictures and videos we took in the apartment, and you can see orbs flying around and weird white misty shadows in the pictures.

"I contacted a paranormal team to see if they could help, and they came down and started their investigation. I was with them, but had to keep leaving, because I was hearing scary stuff, and their equipment batteries went dead in seconds. The investigation picked up women's voices through the spirit box, and visually they saw a tall shadow walk from the bathroom towards our daughter's room, then to laundry room.

"I have the audio cd, and I heard that after they asked the spirit to say something, you hear creepy music box-like music, and then it said, "Hello." A woman screaming was picked up. He was in the attic and asked where he should go, and it said, "Babies room." The hot spots were my daughter's closet, laundry room, and the spot my son's car seat would have been.

"They also heard whispers on the baby monitor and tapping. Every time a noise was heard on the monitor, the light on it would dim real low like it was using the energy from it to talk. We also had light bulbs blow almost daily. Our batteries would be dead daily, too, even brand new batteries were dead in a day.

"The audio also picked up the spirit repeating the investigator's name, and a bunch of other stuff. You need to really listen close. The team decided to cleanse the place, but said the female spirit is not ready to go anywhere, so stuff will start up again. They agreed she was considerate towards my kids. My daughter, at our parents' house, would tell us she misses her friend Green Mommy.

"She told us a few times (it's impossible for a 2yr old to repeat this exactly the same, multiple times) that the Green Mommy was from the train station in the woods, and wanted to take her there, and that there was candy there. We were so scared after hearing that, we never went back with the kids. I would go to pack with friends, and we now live in another place.

"The investigation also had another piece of equipment that picked up words and would repeat them. They picked up 'light mommy' (I'm guessing the spirit called my wife light mommy and she was Green Mommy, I dunno), 'muse' (we had music playing daily almost all day and would dance around, maybe the spirit loved music since muse is music related), the name Paul, 'highway,' and a couple others I forgot. I did my research and found out Pine Bush had a railway that went through it, which made sense as my daughter was saying Green Mommy is from the train station in the woods. And there used to be a large path people walked they called the highway, and was very dangerous as a lot of people were robbed and killed there.

"I don't know what to make of everything that has happened. I can't dismiss anything, because I saw and heard these things. There is now a woman and son living there, and I feel I should warn them. I don't want anyone to go through what we did. Have you heard any stories similar to mine? It sucks not having anyone to talk to or not having any answers. Needless to say, me and my wife are very paranoid now."

While I am not an advocate for spirit boxes, all of the things that Bill and his family saw and heard certainly provided an impressive list of evidence. And while many children have imaginary friends, I think Green Mommy is just a little too creepy to be the product of a two-year-old's imagination. It all sounded compelling enough that I wanted to bring Barbara on a 'drive-by reading,' as I called it. As we would not have access to the interior of the building, I was hoping she would be able to get an idea of what was happening by just looking at the house.

We had dinner at our usual place, *Pure City*, then got in my car and headed to the address Bill had given me. The only thing I told Barb was that someone thought his house was haunted and I wanted her to see it. I gave her no details, and didn't even tell her the street where the house was located, so she would have no prior knowledge.

We were talking and laughing as I drove, until I was just a short distance from where I would be turning onto the street. Barb suddenly grabbed her chest, and I was worried that something was wrong with her, but she said it was just something she was sensing from wherever we were going. As we approached the house, she just had horrible feelings. We parked across the street for a minute, but she didn't want to stay.

Barb believes that a man murdered a woman in that house, possibly by stabbing her in the chest. He may also have kept her captive there for a while before killing her. I haven't been able to find any recent police accounts or newspaper articles about such a crime, but given that the phantom figures appear dressed in old-style clothing (like a tall man who seems to be wearing "a top hat like Abe Lincoln"), these events could have taken place long ago in structures that are long gone.

When I relayed what Barb sensed to Bill, he recalled a strange incident. Soon after moving in, his landlord had hinted that the former tenant had done something in the apartment that required a lot of special cleaning. A few days later, Bill saw a police car pull up in front of the house, and the former tenant was with the police. Had this man committed some sort of crime here, or was there some mundane legal dispute with the landlord?

Until further evidence emerges, it is all speculation. The one thing that *is* certain, is that Bill and his family were haunted by *something*—something so terrifying that it made them flee their home in Pine Bush.

Desmond House
Newburgh, New York

All photos courtesy of Duane Smith.

In April of 2014, I spoke at the Desmond Campus in Newburgh, New York, which is now the location of the continuing education programs for Mount St. Mary's College. The property had once been the site of the original Balmville School, and then became the estate of Thomas C. Desmond, a successful engineer and State Senator. In 1923, he married Alice Curtis, who became an accomplished and successful artist, photographer, and author. In addition to their beautiful home (which they called Krans Kop), Desmond created an arboretum with 850 varieties of trees and shrubs, many of which still exist throughout the extensive grounds.

Two years after Desmond passed away in 1972, Alice—at the age of 79—married former U.S. Congressman Hamilton Fish III—age 87!—of the prestigious Fish family of New York, but that ended in divorce in 1984. When Alice passed away in 1991, she bequeathed the estate to Mount St. Mary's College, which has made wonderful use of the house for the arts and education.

I didn't know anything of its history or occupants when I arrived that evening, but my curiosity would certainly be piqued when I entered the house. I arrived early to set up my PowerPoint presentation, and as it turned out, the guard was just leaving, so I was completely alone when I stepped inside the house—at least on the surface I appeared to be alone. However, I have been in enough haunted houses over the last 20 years to know when spirits are present, and I hadn't gone more than a couple of steps when I went on full alert.

The feeling was so strong that I automatically said, "Hello" to them, and then had to laugh at my instinctive reaction. They weren't scary or threatening, but I certainly got the impression I was walking into *their* house and *they* wanted me to know it. Things did get a little more uncomfortable when I had to get into the small, old elevator to bring my boxes of books upstairs. I couldn't find the light, so I was in total darkness, and I most definitely felt like I had company along for the ride.

However, once I became preoccupied with setting up the computer and projector, and people began filing in, my attention shifted and I was focused solely on my presentation on Hudson Valley UFOs. But that attention shifted once again when everyone left and I was speaking with Sandy Brandman, one of the members of the staff. I asked her about the history of the house, and whether or not they had experienced any paranormal activity. I also told her about psychic Barbara Roth Bleitzhofer, and said I would love to come back with Barb for an investigation.

In the meantime, Sandy showed me around the house, which for the most part was lovely and charming. I say for the most part, because I encountered some incredibly bad wall paper in two small rooms—one was an explosion of pink roses, and the other was poodles on a black background. Oh, the horror!

It wasn't hard to imagine how beautiful this place must have been when the Desmonds were in residence, and extravagant meals were followed by leisurely strolls through the gardens. However, neither Thomas nor Alice were members of the idle rich, as both had long, productive, and varied careers, and also traveled extensively. Alice summed it up when she said she had lived a good, long life, and while certainly not perfect, she had a lot to be thankful for over the years.

I think it was mostly Alice I was sensing that night, but there was a distinct male presence, as well, among possibly several others. But that was where my limited abilities ended, and I knew it was just where Barb's amazing gifts would be able to pick up and run with it.

We arranged to meet with the staff at the Desmond House one afternoon in June, but that morning I was walloped by a migraine headache, something that has plagued me since I was a kid. I called Barb to tell her I couldn't make it, and she agreed to go without me. Fortunately, she was able to get her friend, Duane Smith, to join her to take pictures. Duane has been on several ghost investigations with us over the years, and he is also very sensitive to the spirit world. So as I curled up into the fetal position in a dark, quiet room to ride out the effects of the migraine, I knew the investigation would be in good hands.

Barb recorded everything for me from the minute she arrived, and her first entry was to say that during the drive, she was taking notes of things she was already sensing about the place. The predominant thing was the name Thomas. Of course, the owner of the house was Thomas Desmond—but she didn't know that, as I hadn't told her anything. So she was off to a great start, and she hadn't even arrived yet! She also heard "a woman crying for babies," which may relate to the fact that Thomas and Alice never had children. Alice's strong desire for children would crop up again and again throughout the house.

Photos of Alice and Thomas Desmond.

When Barb and Duane arrived, they took a short walk around the lawn and they both were already feeling "a bit lightheaded and shaky" from the intensity of activity. Right away, Barb could "see the woman who originally owned the place walking the grounds," although she also felt that the woman eventually had difficulty with her legs and could no longer walk. (Alice Desmond did end up in a wheelchair because of crippling arthritis.) She also felt the "cupola on top of the building was a place of mourning."

For the rest of the recordings, Barb would address me directly as if I was there. For example, when they first went inside she said, "We are now inside the Desmond House. I have to tell you, Linda, this place is wild…and here again I get the name Thomas. The name just keeps coming up. He must have been strong-willed."

At this point, they were joined by Desmond staff members Joan McAdam, Sandy Brandman, Jenn Laubach, Tom Fazio, and Jackie Gerace. They all began in the dining room where a strong male spirit used to "hold court." This powerful man was not happy that Barb and Duane were there, as "he didn't believe in this and didn't like this" and wanted them to leave. I found that quite amusing that a spirit didn't believe in people with the psychic ability to sense and communicate with spirits! So many ghosts are in denial!

This man also insisted "this was *his* home, and it would always be *his* home," but he did like the fact that the place was now being used for the arts. It was at this point that one the ladies mentioned Tom Desmond, so Barb was able to confirm the name Thomas. Barb assured them that they had nothing to fear from Thomas, but he was always present somewhere in the house—a belief that was shared by at least one of the women.

"The beauty of it all!" Barb suddenly exclaimed, reiterating what she was hearing from Thomas and Alice in regards to their lovely home and property.

In the library, which Thomas declared was "the *man's* library," Barb at first heard the name Barry, but after repeating it several times—as she often does as more information comes in—it changed to Barry More, then Barrymore.

"He wants me to mention the Barrymores," Barb said, as I wondered if a member of the famous Barrymore family of actors—Lionel, Ethel, and John—had attended one the Desmond parties, or had been a house guest?

"We're going upstairs now, Linda. It feels very heavy."

They went into Thomas' office, where Barb said he had felt the great weight of his responsibilities, and that he regretted all the "collaborations" and compromises that he was forced to make over the years. This, of course, all makes perfect sense for a New York State Senator. What politician has not had to bend to the demands of his position?

When they entered the master bedroom, Barb heard Alice saying, "It is the master bedroom, but the master didn't always sleep here." She then heard Alice crying again, as she had been lonely because her husband was gone quite often. In her autobiographical book, *Yankees and Yorkers*, Alice also mentioned that the two years after Tom's death were very sad and lonely.

Perhaps these feelings could also be connected with her second husband, Hamilton Fish, as that relationship was certainly strained and they divorced after eight years. In *Yankees and Yorkers*, she simply writes that after their marriage in Bermuda, they, "returned to Newburgh and began what we hoped would be happy old age together. It wasn't to be..."

Barb explaining to the group the information she was sensing.

One of the ladies then reminded Barb that when she first arrived, she had talked about "pink walls...lots of pink." Leading Barb to a small room, she turned on the light to reveal the hideous pink rose wallpaper that I had seen on my visit.

"Holy moley!" Barb exclaimed. "I found my pink, Linda!"

Barb then went into some of the offices and commented on the people who worked there, accurately describing both their jobs and personal characteristics. In one of the offices, Barb felt that it had been where the cook—who had a foreign accent—had lived.

They also went up to the cupola, where Barb felt Alice's presence. She was convinced that Alice liked to sit up there and look out across the property. In Alice's former studio, Barb felt her presence most strongly. This is where the spirit of Alice—the artist—is most active.

Alice's former studio.

When I read *Yankees and Yorkers*, I discovered that Alice's first love was painting, but her father only allowed her to study commercial art because it had practical applications. Then came Thomas Desmond, "and after we were married I discovered that he cared little for art and had always wanted to marry a writer. Tom thought writing an ideal occupation for a woman, because it was something she could do in her spare time at home."

So to please her husband, Alice put aside her beloved painting to study writing, and while she became an award-winning author, art was always her first love. It's no wonder that her old studio is her favorite place in the house—now that there aren't any men telling her what to do!

"Alice really likes the music that is played up here," Barb said. "She finds it very soothing. Does someone play something up here, like a cello?"

"I play the viola, and I practice in this room," one of the ladies confirmed.

"She really likes you," Barb said.

At this point, Barb talked at length about the people who worked here, and how Alice and Thomas feel about the various staff members and the events that take place. Listening to all of this, I realized that these two spirits are very much conscious and engaged with everything that goes on here, to a remarkable degree!

The group then went to the cemetery which is on the grounds, containing family members from the small community of houses that stood in this area for generations. Duane started to take pictures, but after just a few photos the camera battery went dead. There is definitely activity around this cemetery, and around the property, as well; not all of which is connected with the Desmonds. When they first arrived, Duane commented that, "Others were here before on this land," and it is some of those "others"—perhaps even some in the cemetery—that can still be felt today.

As they all walked back to the house, Barb had a wonderful feeling from Alice, who she believed used to love walking barefoot through the grass. Here was a woman who led a long, active life of wealth, privilege, and fame, yet one of her greatest pleasures was to just kick off her shoes and feel her toes in the cool grass.

Perhaps the best things in life are free, and the best people are free-spirited…

Copy this page to use for your own ghost hunt. If you know of a haunted site you think should be considered for an upcoming book, please contact me at:

P.O. Box 192, Blooming Grove, NY, 10914

www.ghostinvestigator.com

Field Report

Date: **Location:**

Time In: **Weather:**

Names of People Interviewed:

Equipment: Camera ☐ **Video** ☐ **Audio Recorder**
☐ **Thermometer**   **Other:**

Experiences: Sounds ☐   **Odors** ☐   **Cold Spots** ☐

Visuals ☐ **Touch/Sensations** ☐ **Movement** ☐

Details (Attach extra sheet if necessary):

Time Out: **Total Time on Site:**

Conclusions:

Prepared and Signed by:

Witness(es):

Other books by Linda Zimmermann
Available in print and as e-books
For more info and to order autographed copies:
www.gotozim.com

Dead Center
A Ghost Hunter Novel

When one of the country's largest shopping centers is built in Virginia, rumors abound that the place is haunted by ghosts of Civil War soldiers. Ghost hunter Sarah Brooks must uncover the truth, and come face to face with the restless spirits that walk through the *Dead Center*:

Okay, Sarah Brooks. This is what you do, she said to herself. *This is who you are.*

Closing her eyes, Sarah spun around and counted to three. When she opened her eyes, she had to clamp her hand over her mouth to stifle a scream. There was a pale, misty shape of a man drawing closer. It was like an image being projected into a fog, and it rippled, wavered, then slowly began to take on a more defined shape. The wounded man behind her screamed as if Death himself was coming to take him…

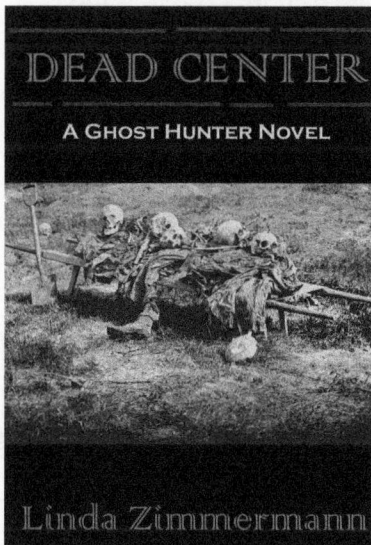

Ghost Investigator Series

Ghost Investigator Volume 1:
Hauntings of the Hudson Valley

Ghost Investigator Volume 2:
From Gettysburg to Lizzie Borden

Ghost Investigator Volume 3

Ghost Investigator Volume 4:
Ghosts of New York and New Jersey

Ghost Investigator Volume 5:
From Beyond the Grave

Ghost Investigator Volume 6:
Dark Shadows

Ghost Investigator Volume 7:
Psychic Impressions

Ghost Investigator Volume 8:
Back Into the Light

Ghost Investigator Volume 9:
Back from the Dead

Ghost Investigator Volume 10

Ghost Investigator Volume 11

Ghost Investigator 10th Anniversary Special Edition:
Favorite Haunts

Ghosts of Rockland County:
Collected Stories Edition

Hudson Valley Haunts: Historic Driving Tours

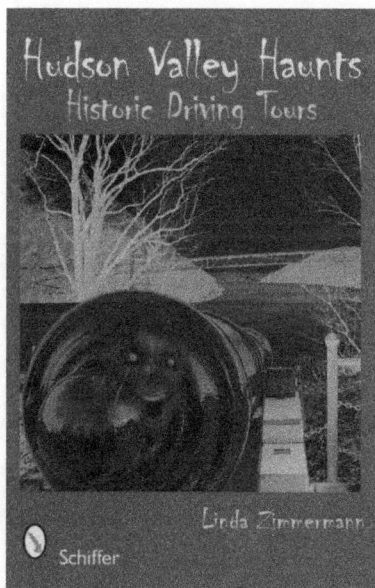

New York's Hudson River Valley is a place of captivating beauty and fascinating history. It is also one of the most haunted regions in the country. From ancient Indian spirits at Spook Rock, to soldiers still walking the battlefield of Fort Montgomery, to the many haunted houses that line the streets of the old Dutch settlements in New Paltz and Hurley, this book has something extra to offer tourists—ghosts that still make their presence known to those who dare to visit.

What greater adventure can there be then to go to such a site, explore the rich history of its people and the events, and then see if you can discover any deeper secrets from the other world, where a passing shadow or faint whisper may signal that you have just had an encounter in the haunted Hudson Valley.

America's Historic Haunts

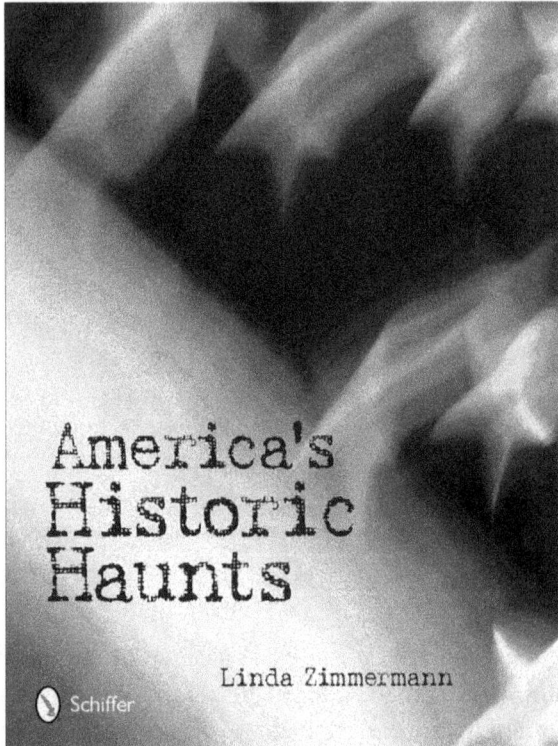

From remote villages in Alaska, to ancient Native American settlements in the southwest, to an old Spanish town in Florida, and bustling metropolitan areas in the northeast, follow the fascinating trail of historic haunts across the country. Test your ghost hunting skills in an old prison or fort, dine in restaurants where paranormal activity is on the menu, and sleep in some of America's most haunted inns. Whether you're a frequent flier or an armchair adventurer, this book will take you on a journey of discovery into the people, places, and events that led to the spirits that still walk among us in some of this country's greatest travel destinations.

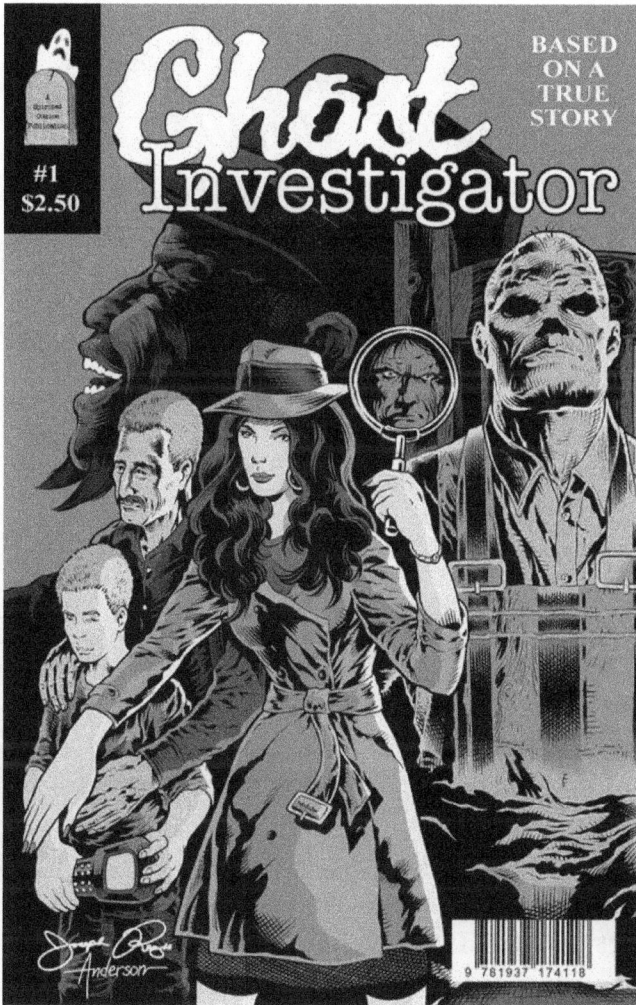

Ghost Investigator
The Comic Book
Issue #1

Available at: www.comicfleamarket.com

Issue #2 coming soon!

In the Night Sky
and
Hudson Valley UFOs

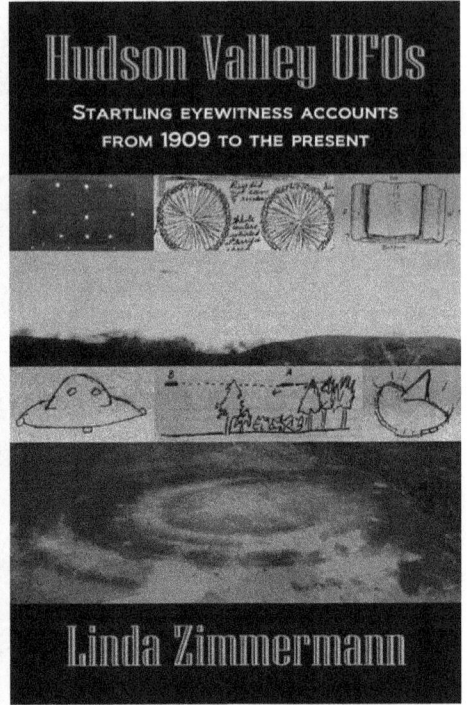

Eyewitness accounts of classic flying saucers, giant, silent triangles, and possible abductions in one of the most active UFO areas of the country.

The film *In the Night Sky: I Recall a UFO* based on the book was the winner of the People's Choice Award at the EBE Film Festival at the 2013 International UFO Congress.

HVZA and HVZA 2:
Hudson Valley Zombie Apocalypse

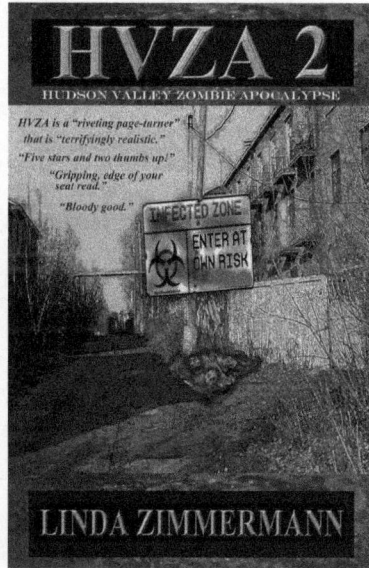

Amazon.com Reviews:

"GREAT book. Buy it; you won't regret it. Well... except maybe for at 3 AM when you're either A) still up reading because can't put this page-turner down or B) waking up out of a zombie nightmare because the characters and situations in the book can seem so REAL. But buy it anyway."

"You relate, you get sucked in, seriously it's been a while since I enjoyed a book so much."

"The author has an uncanny ability to pull you into the story and make you feel like you are there."

"Zimmermann really hits home with her depiction of life during the collapse of civilization, and the heart wrenching losses, choices and sacrifices that people must make in order to survive. Zimmermann is a master manipulator of emotions: the love, fear, sadness, pain, and suffering of the various characters are surprisingly real. Set in the Hudson Valley, the authentic locations and settings lend an additional layer of realism that so many other works of fiction neglect. These just are not zombies that are attacking people - these are zombies that are attacking your neighbors and family and friends."

HVZA:
Hudson Valley Zombie Apocalypse

THE GRAPHIC NOVEL

HVZA
Hudson Valley Zombie Apocalypse

Based on the novel by
Linda Zimmermann

Project Director
Don E. Smith, Jr.

Art Director & Cover
Nick Mockoviak

"A truly imaginative
Zombie Anthology.
Full of stories for
every appetite."
- Paul J. Salamoff
Writer/Producer

"A truly imaginative Zombie Anthology. Full of stories for every appetite."
-- Paul J. Salamoff, Writer/Producer (Discord, Logan's Run: Last Day)

"Not since peanut butter and chocolate has there been as perfect a combination as zombies and comics! What's better than one zombie story? How about a whole brain-eating collection of zombie stories?!"
--Jim Salicrup, Editor-in-Chief, Papercutz and former Marvel Comics editor on "The Avengers," "The Amazing Spider-Man," "The Uncanny X-Men" and "The Fantastic Four."

Bad Science:
A Brief History of Bizarre Misconceptions, Totally Wrong Conclusions, and Incredibly Stupid Theories

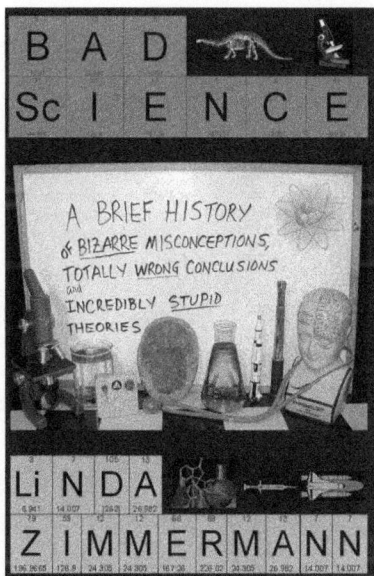

Winner of the 2011 Silver Medal for Humor
in the international Independent Publisher Awards

Amazon.com Review:

"*Bad Science* is simultaneously informative and ever-so-entertaining. Riveting! Enthralling! Hilarious! I highly recommend this book if you like a jaw dropping read that is a LAUGH OUT LOUD."

WWW.GOTOZIM.COM

www.ingramcontent.com/pod-product-compliance
Lightning Source LLC
Chambersburg PA
CBHW032141040426
42449CB00005B/355